754

ABE 8353

√81-1242 $7.95   OP
658
Wachs
The successful manager's guide

26 T

1/10

24 TR
2009

4/11

The Successful Manager's Guide

William Wachs

PARKER PUBLISHING COMPANY, INC.

West Nyack, New York

Second Printing.....February, 1969

What This Book Will Do for You

OVER-ALL BENEFITS TO YOU

1. It will show you how to be a more successful manager.
2. It will give you specific techniques for becoming more successful.
3. It will give you a simple and direct standard for evaluating your present techniques and seeing where you can improve them for your own and your company's benefit.
4. It will provide you with yet another opportunity to continue developing your own management philosophy and skills.
5. It will broaden your management scope.

SPECIFIC BENEFITS TO YOU

You will learn new and more profitable techniques of direct and immediate applicability to your own responsibilities in the following management areas:

- How to get continuing maximum/optimum profitability out of your subordinates.
- How to get along with your superiors while doing for them exactly what they want from you.
- How to get the greatest/best cooperation from your colleagues while giving them the same.
- How to organize and run your own management workflow for greatest effectiveness with greatest peace of mind.
- How to be a greater management success each day than you were the day before.

SPECIFIC TECHNIQUES YOU WILL LEARN

—How to communicate more effectively with your subordinates, your colleagues and your superiors.

—How to train your subordinates with a minimum of effort and a maximum of results.

—How to plan your work with the greatest of ease and the best of results.

—How to motivate your subordinates to exert themselves constantly to their greatest and best capacities along lines laid down by you.

—How to supervise your subordinates with the greatest effectiveness and the smoothest relationships.

—How to follow up most profitably on the results of your supervision.

—How to get the most out of the time you spend on your own paperwork.

—How to remember "automatically" what you don't want to forget.

—How to get your job done and still enjoy your work.

—How to do by yourself only those things which cannot properly be delegated.

SELF-DEVELOPMENT YOU WILL UNDERGO

This book will take your job as it should be and break it down into its basic elements.

Self-Development Idea Number One: You will have a continuing guide to a practicable, profitable approach to planning and organizing your daily responsibilities.

For each basic element of your job the book will present one or more "tried-and-true" successful techniques for tackling and mastering the tasks involved.

Self-Development Idea Number Two: You will have at your disposal either a new technique or a variation of one you've been using all along. In applying the new one, or varying the old one, you will be getting a new look at yourself and trying new or different ways to solve old problems. This will bring you along still further toward your managerial self-fulfillment until you get to the point where you can become and stay objective all the time, and innovate where necessary.

Accompanying each technique there will be one or more actual cases from the author's wide and varied experience in businesses of all kinds and sizes all over the country. Each case will provide an actual illustration of how one or more managers in jobs like yours failed because they didn't apply effectively the technique under discussion, or succeeded because they did use it properly.

Self-Development Idea Number Three: As you read the illustrative cases you will automatically think of many situations you've already been in, are in now or will probably experience. You'll be stimulated to evaluate how you handled such experiences, how you could have done better or what you'll do if the occasion arises. This will sharpen your ability to be self-analytical and self-critical. It will also give you a further opportunity to study the close relationship between accepted principles of sound management and the actual down-to-earth happenings where they should be practiced. This will help show you how closely you are approaching the ideal goal: to solve day-to-day problems as quickly as possible, with maximum practicality and greatest assurance of accuracy and correctness.

DOLLARS AND CENTS YOU WILL EARN

Every word in this book reaches for greater profit for you and your company, both immediate and long-range. You can read each *Success Factor* in it in an hour or two. Even before you reread any one page, or study it more carefully, you will already know how you can earn more money for your company. And you will be well on the way toward seeing how your improved management techniques will ultimately mean more money for you in the form of a larger check.

The Steps to Success

The First Success Challenge
MAXIMIZE YOUR MANAGERIAL POTENTIAL

Success Factor
Number One   **How You Can Guarantee Profitable Accountability** .   PAGE **19**

> *Guarantee continuing profitability; marshal human resources; pinpoint the management team; recognize non-management differences from management; fulfill your responsibility, authority and accountability; inventory your organizational relationships; practice teamwork for profit.*

Success Factor
Number Two   **How You Can Increase Your Successability** .   .   **29**

> *Recognize your management assets: knowledge, attitudes, skills, habits; realize your inherent abilities; develop the many acquirable qualifications; build on what you have; inventory your assets; know what you need; find out where to get it; exert the necessary effort; plan your time; emphasize self-improvement; apply what you learn; continually evaluate yourself; keep on improving; be confident of success.*

Success Factor
Number Three   **How You Can Follow the Best Road to Profit** .   .   **41**

> *Make company objectives your own; help produce profit; practice effective cost control; increase profitable productivity; promote other company goals—reputation, service, interest in employees, personal satisfactions.*

Success Factor
Number Four   **How You Can Turn Paper Work into Paper Money** .   **51**

> *Assess your paper work habits; become self-disciplined and orderly; divide papers into active and passive; organize your office facilities; keep facilities orderly; make your memory "automatic"; always strive for efficiency.*

The Second Success Challenge   PAGE
MAXIMIZE YOUR MANAGERIAL RELATIONSHIPS

Success Factor
Number Five   **How to Work Effectively with Your Boss** **69**

> *Meet your boss more than half-way; find out what he expects of you; find out how to do this successfully; line up needed facilities; make your own decisions; solve your own problems; be available to your boss; make only wise decisions; keep your boss informed; be where he wants you, and when; treat your boss right; do successfully everything he expects of you.*

Success Factor
Number Six   **How You Can Get Along with Your Colleagues** . . **85**

> *Know your "line and staff" relationships; follow the line properly; deal appropriately with "staff-related" colleagues; take the proper initiative in team-work; get along well with your colleagues; follow through tactfully on cooperation provided to you; meet your lateral promises; limit your "staff" suggestions; be receptive to the suggestions of others.*

Success Factor
Number Seven   **How You Can Successfully Man Your Department** . . **99**

> *Make an inventory of the people you need; recruit early and often; anticipate future manpower needs; line up potential candidates; plan manpower in depth; decide on your best span of control.*

Success Factor
Number Eight   **How You Can Delegate without Losing Control** . . **109**

> *Delegate everything you possibly can; keep on being responsible; delegate all commensurate authority; keep a record of what you delegate; check up on the progress of the work; don't wait until deadlines are reached.*

The Third Success Challenge
MAXIMIZE YOUR PRODUCTIVITY

Success Factor
Number Nine   **How You Can Control Your Productivity** **121**

> *Every management level is important to profit; Management must assure profit through Non-Management; profit comes from the proper balance between costs and results; do only those things whose cost is consistent with profits; you're responsible for your subordinates' profitability; results must be of satisfactory quantity and quality; even quality must be quantified; time affects cost; productivity must cost no more than absolutely necessary; pay careful attention to safety and housekeeping; don't damage morale through unnecessary changes.*

Success Factor
Number Ten   **How You Can Make Productivity Profitable** . . . **137**

> *Your subordinates' profitable productivity depends on their: knowing what's expected of them, knowing how to do it, having all of the necessary facilities, wanting to do their best; you must assure this through effective communications, training, planning, motivation, supervision and followup.*

Success Factor
Number Eleven   **How You Can Keep Your Men Profitably Informed** . **153**

> *Make sure your subordinates know what's expected of them; convey standards to them; quantify all of their requirements; tell them that they must manage their subordinates; tell them when they come to you; help them develop themselves; look for your replacement; tell your subordinates the controls you'll use; communicate in depth; check up on your depth-communication effectiveness.*

Success Factor
Number Twelve   **How You Can Communicate Profitable "How-To"** . **171**

> *Decide who needs what training; plan training well in advance; insist on complete understanding and full agreement; check up soon and often; train in depth.*

The Steps to Success

The Fourth Success Challenge
MAXIMIZE YOUR PEOPLE—MOTIVATION

Success Factor   PAGE
Number Thirteen **How You Can Plan Successful Motivation** **181**

> *Know your subordinates' capacities; get them to exert themselves fully; know who always wants to do his best; encourage them to keep it up; know who needs outside stimulation; give it to them.*

Success Factor
Number Fourteen **How You Can Get the Most Out of Your Men** . . . **191**

> *Get your subordinates to exert themselves fully; set the motivation "stage" properly; know who are the Self-Motivators; use motivations wisely; offer more money where feasible; relate money to minimum acceptable performance; indicate penalties for less than minimum; emphasize job security; relate it to performance; make your people care about you; appeal to psychic-satisfaction motivations; offer promotion-opportunities wisely; follow up on motivation; get after the laggards; motivate in depth.*

Success Factor
Number Fifteen **How You Can Supervise Successfully** **209**

> *Check up on your subordinates; supervise them effectively and frequently; find out what's going on; select the best methods for supervising; emphasize frequent physical supervision; find out what's going on and why; decide on followup; evaluate your subordinates; keep morale high; be natural and subtle; supervise in depth; respect levels of authority and responsibility.*

Success Factor
Number Sixteen **How You Can Profitably Follow Up on Supervision** **225**

> *Follow up on all supervision; check up on the effectiveness of your followup; follow up both among and away from your people; document carefully and fully; make decisions arising from supervision; carry your decisions out promptly; praise and/or reward where merited; warn or discipline where warranted; follow up on followup; follow up in depth.*

The First Success Challenge

Maximize Your Managerial Potential

How You Can
Guarantee Profitable
Accountability

This *Success Factor* helps you fulfill your major obligation to your company: to assure a continuingly-satisfactory *Profit* through your own efforts and those of your subordinates.

It emphasizes two basic concepts:

1. The fact that you're accountable; and
2. What you're accountable for.

ACCEPT YOUR ACCOUNTABILITY

You must constantly produce the results you're responsible for through your:

- Thinking
- Words
- Actions

When you do, you deserve the credit. Where, however, you fall short of what your superiors expect of you, you must *answer* to them for your less-than-desirable performance. The blame is squarely on you; the fault is yours alone.

You must suffer the consequences of your poor performance and results. And you must take *every* step possible to remedy the situation and prevent its recurrence.

19

EQUATE ACCOUNTABILITY WITH PROFIT

Here's what you're accountable for:

*P*lanning all of your activities.
*R*allying all resources available to you.
*O*rganizing yourself and others.
*F*ollowing the best paths to success.
*I*nvestigating all possible areas of weakness.
*T*aking all necessary steps to assure success.

PINPOINT ACCOUNTABILITY PEOPLE

You will satisfactorily meet your accountability only if you properly utilize the best efforts of your whole team. To do this effectively you have to know who is available to work with, and to what extent they can be relied on. To judge this you must first fully understand your own role in overall company responsibility.

Analyze the Setup

You could more satisfactorily fulfill your own profit obligations if *all* of the employees you worked with had the same kinds and degrees of:

- Attitudes
- Experience
- Knowledge
- Habits
- Skills

Unfortunately, most companies are made up of *two different* teams, grouped according to the above qualifications. Your organization probably shapes up like the diagram on the following page.

Align the Management Team

You are part of your company's *management team.* To qualify as such you—and all your team-mates—have to be in *either* of these two categories:

1. You have authority over—and are responsible and accountable for —a given number of subordinates.

Examples of people in this category are:

- A superintendent with foremen reporting directly to him.
- A foreman responsible for non-management people.
- A supervisor of clerks in an office.

```
┌─────────────────────────────┐
│                             │
│       MANAGEMENT            │
│                             │
│         TEAM                │
│                             │
├─────────────────────────────┤
│                             │
│                             │
│     NON-MANAGEMENT          │
│                             │
│        PEOPLE               │
│                             │
│                             │
└─────────────────────────────┘
```

2. Your superiors consider you a part of the management team—even if you have no subordinates—because of the high-level responsibilities you've been given.

Examples of people with that kind of responsibility are:

- An assistant to the President.
- A Safety Engineer.
- A Wage and Salary Administrator.
- The Head of Production Control.

Every member of the management team is automatically accountable for continuing maximum/optimum contributions to company profit.

This means that *you* must hold yourself thoroughly accountable to your superiors for suitable profitability. It also means that you have a right to *insist* that your *management* subordinates adopt, feel, and properly fulfill the same kind and degree of accountability.

A Case in Point

Harry Randall is Division Manager of a multi-product manufacturing company. He has three foremen reporting to him. One week, one of them, Bob Leander, failed to meet his production quota. When Harry remonstrated with Bob over this, the foreman said:

"It wasn't my fault. You know the kind of men I've got working for me. If they don't want to follow schedules, they just won't, and you can't make them."

Harry was finally able to convince Bob that:

- He had agreed to the reasonableness of the schedule.
- He had never pointed out to Harry any men whose continued poor performance warranted disciplinary measures or a transfer to different work.
- *He* must have failed somewhere along the line to manage his men properly.

Bob had to admit that he was the *only* one to blame for this failure, and that his responsibility and *accountability* for success was an ever-present prerequisite for membership on the management team.

MAXIMIZE THE EFFORTS OF NON-MANAGEMENT

You may have to deal differently with your *non-management* subordinates. You still have to get the best and the most out of them that you can, but your approach may have to be different. You'll probably have to:

—Realize that there may be very little that you can do about making them feel accountable.

—Find *other* ways of getting from them the kinds of profitable results you want.

Another Case

Mel McCarthy was Office Manager in the headquarters of a many-branched bank. He had some twenty clerks in his charge.

Helen Thomas was strictly non-management. She was, on the whole, conscientious, and capable of doing good routine work.

One day Mel assigned a rather difficult task to Helen. She didn't do it satisfactorily. Mel criticized her for her failure and she burst into tears.

Mel should have found out why she didn't succeed. He'd have discovered that the reason was that the new work was beyond her abilities. He wasn't wise to try to hold her *accountable* for *any* task he might have assigned to her. He should have realized that he'd asked her to go beyond her scope, and should have given her only that kind of job which she could do well.

ASSURE INTER-TEAM COOPERATION

What you'll have to do, in the light of all this, is:

1. Make yourself completely accountable for profit from:
   a. your own efforts; and
   b. the efforts of *all* your subordinates, management and non-management alike.

2. Make sure to get your *management* subordinates to accept and fulfill *their* accountability for profits.

3. Establish and maintain the best kind of cooperation between the management team and non-management, even if the latter won't accept *accountability* for profits.

How will you achieve that goal? Let's talk first about how you and your *management* subordinates can satisfy *your* profit accountability.

MEET "RAA"

You, like all management men, have three basic commitments. The first—accountability—has already been discussed. The other two are *authority* and *responsibility*. And *only* a management man can be expected to meet those three requirements.

You, along with all other management men, must know, understand, accept and satisfactorily fulfill your:

*R*esponsibilities
*A*uthority
*A*ccountability

Let's talk now about your *responsibilities* and your *authority*.

YOU ARE "RESPONSIBLE" FOR PROFIT

You are *accountable* to your superiors (an *upward* obligation) for knowing, understanding, accepting and satisfactorily meeting your *responsibilities* (a *downward* obligation).

I define *responsibility* as an *absolute* obligation to understand and successfully complete all aspects of a Manager's job. It is this word *absolute* which distinguishes the word *responsibility* (used only to describe *management* duties) from *obligation, duty, task* (or any other word used by itself) which applies to *non-management* people.

Compare Responsibility to Mere Obligation

You will more clearly understand and fulfill the requirements of your position if you follow these distinctions:

A management man	A non-management man
Has to agree that he must meet *all* of his commitments: completely, accurately and profitably.	May or may not be willing—or able—to do well *all* of the duties or tasks assigned to him.
Is *part of management, only* because he *can* and *will* succeed in all of his responsibilities.	Can still be retained in his job even if he falls down periodically on some of his obligations.

MEET YOUR RESPONSIBILITIES PROPERLY

You are responsible for:
- Your own productivity; and
- Your subordinates' productivity.

Boost Your Boss

Your boss has the right to say to you:

"I'd like you to take care of this and send it to me, fully and satisfactorily complete, by Friday of this week."

Unless you need more time, and can convince him of that fact, it's your *responsibility* to have it in his hands exactly as he wants it, not later than that day.

If some unforeseen obstacle comes up before then, tell your boss about it at once and make the necessary adjustment in the schedule. But, barring such a contingency, you'll want to deliver the results where they belong, in tip-top shape, *on the button.*

If not, what does he need you for? Isn't that what he's paying you for? That's why you're part of the Management Team.

Adjust to Non-Management

Contrast the above with a situation involving non-management fulfillment of an obligation.

Suppose you ask a non-management subordinate to do a particular task, according to certain specifications, and have it ready by tomorrow.

When the next day arrives and he hasn't done it—completely or satisfactorily—what can you do about it?

Bawl him out? That may cause him to adopt an attitude which would make him less or more poorly productive from there on in.

Fire him? While there are times and circumstances when such action is justified, you may be better off accepting what you can get from your non-management men, always trying—of course—to increase and improve their productivity.

A Relevant Anecdote

An American diplomat in West Berlin was visiting a friend who operated a restaurant there. While they were both seated at a table, a waiter approached to take their order. When the waiter had gone back into the kitchen, the following conversation took place at the table:

The Diplomat: Don't you know that that waiter is an East Berlin spy?
The Restaurateur: Of course I do!
The Diplomat: Then, why don't you fire him?
The Restaurateur: Because if I do, the next Communist spy they send me may not be such an efficient waiter!

EXERCISE YOUR "AUTHORITY" FOR PROFIT

You have full authority to undertake, carry out and enforce *all* of your responsibilities. If you haven't been told so expressly, *assume* that you have such authority. You'll find that your boss intends you to have it.

Authority is the *right* and *power* to:
—Issue appropriate orders.
—Provide necessary facilities and manpower.
—Make correct decisions and be backed up for them.
—Evaluate the performance of the people to whom you have issued orders.
—Play a major role in the process of rewarding and disciplining people according to their contributions to getting the work done.

Recognize Your Authority

Authority is a *management* term, exclusively, just as *responsibility* and *accountability* are.

You want your *non-management* people to exercise discretion, judgment and initiative, within prescribed limits, but they should not be given or allowed to practice any *authority*.

You Must Exercise Your Authority

Authority is not just a privilege. It's a *responsibility*. You *have* the power to give and enforce orders and make decisions. But you *must exercise* that power wisely and properly *for every one of your responsibilities*.

Avoid This Pitfall

I came across a particularly flagrant example, in a brewery, of failure to exercise authority.

The established procedure for handling cases of repeated non-management unwillingness to meet productivity requirements was an "Unsatisfactory Performance Report." After a first, oral warning, properly documented, subsequent failures to do what was expected were supposed to result in the preparation of such a form. This was to be signed by the workman involved and his foreman, and filed with the Industrial Relations Manager.

In meetings I held with the foreman and their superiors, many complaints were voiced about the continued poor performance of some of the men. Many of the complaints were against repeaters.

But, in the few years preceding my contact with that company, *only three* Unsatisfactory Performance Reports had ever been prepared and filed by the foremen.

REMEMBER YOUR ACCOUNTABILITY

Let's re-examine your *accountability* in the light of our discussion of *responsibility* and *authority*.

—You are *accountable* for the proper and continuing fulfillment of every one of your *responsibilities* and all of your *authority*.

—Your *major accountability* is for assuring continuing, desired profit from your own efforts and those of all your subordinates.

—Accountability is a strictly *management* concept: you and your management subordinates can't escape it; you can't really expect it from non-management, but *you* are accountable for *their* proper fulfillment of *their* obligations.

INVENTORY YOUR ACCOUNTABILITY RELATIONSHIPS

You will, of course, constantly have to work with others in the company in the fulfillment of your accountability commitments. The most effective way to begin your undertaking of such cooperation is to make a "Relationship Inventory."

Accompanying is a graphic representation of the relationships any management man may find himself in. Look for your spot on the accompanying diagram and plan your program of inter-position teamwork.

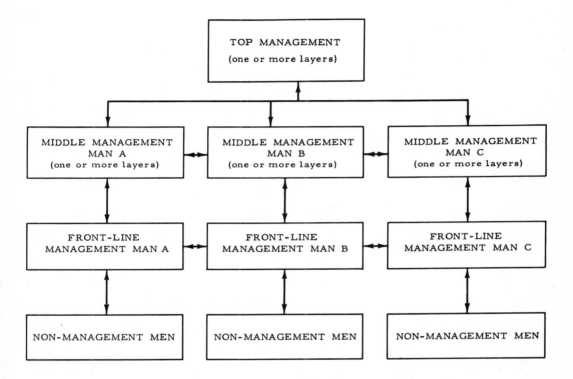

SUCCESS CAPSULE NUMBER ONE

This *Success Factor* has introduced the basic concepts and assumptions on which you will build your increased management success:

1. Your major obligation to your company is to *guarantee* continuing maximum/optimum profitability from your own efforts and from those of your subordinates.
2. You must effectively marshal all available human resources—your own as well as those of all the other people you work with—in order to achieve your profit goals constantly.
3. You must recognize *who* is available for this cooperation, and on *what team* he is.

    a. This requires you to accept the fact that there are differences between management and non-management people, which go to the essence of how they will cooperate with you.

    b. You are an important member of the *Management Team;* all of you on that team *must* guarantee profit; you are *automatically* "accountable" for such profit.

    c. Those who are *not* on the Management Team *can* be directed toward desirable profitability, but the approach is different from that used with *management* people.

4. As an important member of your company's Management Team, you must understand, assume and satisfactorily fulfill your *RAA:* responsibility, authority and accountability.

    a. Responsibility (an *absolute* downward obligation to do consistently well what's expected) is a strictly *management* concept, and is therefore a very important part of your job.

    b. Authority (the right or power to make decisions and enforce your responsibilities) is also strictly a *management* concept, but it is a *responsibility* as well as a right.

    c. You *must* exercise proper *authority* for every *responsibility* you have.

    d. Accountability is an *upward* obligation.

5. Know your place on the management chart and inventory the relationships you must establish and maintain in order to practice continuing *Teamwork for Profit.*

How You Can
Increase Your
Successability

This *Success Factor* shows you how you can maximize your abilities and experience. This will help you achieve the management goals you and your position have set for you.

To accomplish this you'll have to take the following *Five Sure-Fire Steps:*

1. Carefully analyze the requirements of your job.
2. Carefully analyze your own abilities and experience.
3. Make an accurate inventory of your management strengths and weaknesses.
4. Do everything necessary to acquire and maintain any strengths you lack.
5. Eliminate important weaknesses.

Now let's begin to follow this path.

ANALYZE FULLY YOUR JOB REQUIREMENTS

First we'll tackle the *basic step.*

As a successful management man you must adequately fulfill, at the very least, the *Four Fundamental Elements* of your job. These represent *"Kash* in the bank" for both you and the company.

29

Utilize Your Kash Wisely

Here's what your *Kash* consists of:

- *K*nowledge of what your job calls for.
- *A*ttitudes of the right kind toward your work, your company and its people.
- *S*kills for successfully handling assigned responsibilities and people.
- *H*abits of effective work and relations.

Make a Kash Inventory

Now you're ready to see how *you* stack up against those measuring rods. As you go along in your analysis, make a *management inventory* of your strengths and weaknesses.

EVALUATE YOUR PRESENT SUCCESS LEVEL

To help you compare your situation with valid criteria, I'm putting these in the form of checklists. As you read the first column in each of the checklists, evaluate your own status regarding each item discussed. Fill in the columns provided for that purpose.

This will serve to guide you in your efforts to increase your strengths and eliminate your weaknesses.

Increase Your Managerial Knowledge

This first checklist is designed to help you evaluate your managerial *knowledge*. You can measure *yourself* against what's generally called for in a man in your position. This will make it easier to *get to know* the significant things you *ought to know*.

My job calls for me to know well	At present I know this				
	Entirely satis- factorily	*Reasonably well*	*In only average fashion*	*In below average fashion*	*As described below*
My company's objectives					
Company policies affecting me					
My place in the company's organizational structure					

My job calls for me to know well	At present I know this				
	Entirely satis- factorily	*Reasonably well*	*In only average fashion*	*In below average fashion*	*As described below*
The nature and extent of my accountability					
My responsibilities and authority					
The technical aspects of my work					
Company procedures affecting me					
The areas of collateral teamwork expected of me					
The facilities at my disposal					
The people I'm sup- posed to work with					

IMPROVE YOUR MANAGEMENT ATTITUDES

Before discussing this element of job fulfillment, let's make sure we both use our terms in the same way. Experience shows that many people give the word *attitude* a different meaning from the one intended here.

They often say: "I don't like your attitude." What they really mean is: "I don't like the *manifestations* of your attitude that I see."

Understand the Meaning of "Attitude"

The word *attitude* is used here to refer to an *internal* reaction to people, situations, things, problems, etc. This reaction can be the result of stimuli from the outside (for instance, something someone says to you). Or, it can come from something within you (heartburn).

It can be caused predominantly by an emotion, such as unreasoning fear. Or it can stem partly from an emotion and partly from a rational reaction. (For example, a man may dislike doing paper work partly be- cause he didn't like his elementary-school penmanship teacher. But part of the reason may be that he wants to get out into the shop where the action is.)

Look Within for Attitudes

Whatever its cause, an attitude is strictly something *inside* you. This is so even if you never let anybody know that you *have* that attitude.

And you may have *hundreds* of different attitudes toward different people, situations, etc.

What's more, your attitude *today* toward one particular situation may not be the same as your attitude *tomorrow* regarding that same situation.

Make Your Own Attitude Inventory

Let's see what attitudes you must consistently have, as a bare minimum, in order to be an effective Manager.

Attitudes essential for me as a successful management man	*I'm satisfied that I have this attitude to the proper extent*	*I'm not satisfied with the extent to which I have this attitude*	*I'm not sure (or I don't know) whether I have this attitude to the proper extent*
A sincere desire to make a continuing, maximum/optimum contribution to my company's profit			
A positive feeling of pleasure in working for my company			
A positive feeling of pleasure in working hard			
Great satisfaction at being a member of my company's Management Team			
Willingness to spend all the time needed to do my work well			
Willingness to exert myself constantly to my maximum/optimum capacity			
Willingness to learn as much as I can and must about how to do my job better			

Attitudes essential for me as a successful management man	I'm satisfied that I have this attitude to the proper extent	I'm not satisfied with the extent to which I have this attitude	I'm not sure (or I don't know) whether I have this attitude to the proper extent
Readiness to evaluate myself constantly in order to see whether and/or how I can improve in my work			
Respect for all the people for and with whom I must work			
A proper amount of humility toward others			
Confidence in my own ability to do my work well			
The necessary amount of enthusiasm for my job			
Willingness to make all necessary efforts to get along with others			
Punctuality, promptness and regularity of action			
Willingness to plan and organize myself for my work			
Cooperativeness			
Firmness and consistency tempered with flexibility			
Willingness to compromise			
Patience and calm			
Fairness and objectivity			
A sincere interest in the well-being of others			
Friendliness tempered with the need for the proper distance from my line subordinates			

Attitudes essential for me as a successful management man	*I'm satisfied that I have this attitude to the proper extent*	*I'm not satisfied with the extent to which I have this attitude*	*I'm not sure (or I don't know) whether I have this attitude to the proper extent*
Empathy and sympathy, where appropriate			
Communicativeness tempered by the proper amount of taciturnity			
Willingness to give credit where credit is due			

UPGRADE YOUR PRESENT SKILLS

The third item in your *Kash* account is the skill you bring to the performance of your responsibilities and to the exercise of your authority. Rate yourself on the accompanying test of the minimum skills needed for a successful Manager.

To do my job well I need to have at least the following skills	*I already have these skills to a satisfactory degree of development*	*I'm not satisfied with my present level of development in these skills*	*I'm not sure that I possess these skills to the proper degree of development*
Ability to get along well with others			
Ability to express myself adequately			
Ability to motivate and/ or inspire others			
Ability to judge people accurately			
Ability to control myself			
Skill in making decisions			
Ability to initiate new ideas or activities			
Skill in planning my work			
Technical skills needed in my work			

CHANGE UNSUCCESSFUL HABITS

Now we come to the last line in our listing of management assets: the *habits* you must have and practice in doing your job well. Here's the final, suggested self-evaluation test in this *Success Factor:*

Habits I should have and practice in my job	*I'm satisfied with my status regard-ing those habits*	*I'm not satisfied*	*I'm not sure whether I'm satisfied*
Accuracy and preciseness			
Care in doing things			
Alertness and awareness			
Attentive listening			
Brevity with thoroughness			
Thinking before acting or speaking			
Perseverance			
Proper appearance			
Pleasing personality			
Evaluation of others and myself			
Self-control			
Concealment of attitudes which shouldn't be mani-fested			

USE A POSITIVE APPROACH

Go back over the results of your self-quizzes. You'll note whether you evaluate yourself as having some less-than-satisfactory knowledge, attitudes, skills or habits. If you do, adopt this *Positive Approach:* It's *easy* to over-come *any* of your shortcomings.

Let's see why this is so.

Capitalize on Your "Inheritance"

There are only a few basic traits with which a person is born. These are presented here with an indication of their role in management success, and a clue to how *you* probably already stack up regarding them.

Traits with which a person is born	Their role in management success	How you probably already stack up regarding those traits
Anatomical characteristics	A management man must have no physical defects or problems which could stand in his way in trying to do his job well.	You require no greater degree of anatomical well-being for your present job than you needed for your previous management responsibilities.
Physiological functioning	The body's organs, glands, muscles, etc., must be able to perform in such a way that one can physically and emotionally meet his responsibilities.	You were able to function well in your previous management job. You can, therefore, be sure that you are physiologically capable of doing your present one well.
Intellectual capacity	One must have enough brain power to be able to adjust himself mentally to new situations and learn all that is required for filling his position properly.	You wouldn't have been appointed to your present position if your boss hadn't been confident that you had all the intellectual capacity needed for your current responsibilities.

So it can be seen that you already have all the *inherent* traits needed for the successful accomplishment of your managerial duties. If, then, you feel you have some management weaknesses, you're in a terrific position to do something about them, because they're "acquired" traits.

HARNESS YOUR ACQUIRED TRAITS

Each of us has it within him to change characteristics acquired after birth.

Let's take some typical traits which can stand in the way of a Manager's success.

Technological Limitations

If your job calls for some additional technical knowledge, you can readily acquire it.

A Case in Point

Tom Harris had been Shift Foreman in a factory. When a vacancy occurred, he was made Production Control Manager.

His new duties called for a knowledge of industrial engineering. Tom wasn't a P.E., but he started right in to learn what he needed.

The latest *Manual of Industrial Engineering* and his boss's help soon brought Tom to the required point.

And as he worked on his new job he learned more and more of what was called for.

Ineffective Communications

You may have to talk to a group of men and convince them to go along with you on your plans. Just because you've always experienced "stage fright" doesn't mean you can't overcome it.

An Illustration

Take Pete Carter.

Every time he had to stand up before his subordinates he faltered, stumbled and hesitated. Then he was promoted to the post of Operations Manager of the electric power plant.

He had to conduct periodic meetings with his subordinates. He sought help from a friend of the family who specialized in oral communications.

Practice and experience did the rest. Pete is still no orator, but he gets his message across.

Failure to Delegate

Suppose you've always been accustomed to doing everything yourself. Your new job absolutely requires you to delegate most of your responsibilities to your subordinates. Is your present habit hard to break?

An Example

It was hard for Arthur Hayes, but he overcame it.

He'd been Head Bookkeeper for his stamping company. As such he'd done a good deal of the posting himself.

When he was made Controller he just couldn't go on in the same way as before. With a bit of guidance from the Executive Vice President and plenty of will power, he learned to delegate.

Today he's a real Controller. He has capable bookkeepers doing the posting for him.

Resistance to Change

You may be convinced that there isn't a better way of doing what you've been responsible for over a period of many years. But you may be wrong. And you *can* get into the habit of doing it differently and better.

An Illustration

A model of a very successful and difficult change comes from a Department Store Chain which was rearranging the responsibilities of its Buyers.

These men and women were no longer to have authority over the sale, in the various stores, of the merchandise they bought. This was a difficult pill for them to swallow. It went contrary to the long tradition of their industry.

But most of them made a real effort. Within one year they were cooperating very effectively with the stores' newly-constituted sales-management force.

The Buyers found out that they could really gauge *what* they should *buy* without being in a position to determine *how* it should be *sold*.

KASH IN ON YOUR HIDDEN ASSETS

Let's see where we are now:

- You already have all the anatomical, physiological and intellectual characteristics necessary for you to do your job well.
- Any knowledge, attitudes, skills or habits you need are within your reach. You need only *build* on what the good Lord has given you.

But every builder needs the proper materials, tools and techniques. Here are *Ten Aids to Acquiring the KASH You Need:*

AID NUMBER ONE

Be completely honest with yourself in evaluating your strengths and shortcomings. If you need help in this, consult a reliable colleague or specialist, and be receptive to his analysis. But remember that your *own* judgment must play an important part in your self-critique.

AID NUMBER TWO

Make up your mind that you *can* and *will* acquire the characteristics and/or knowledge you need. Remember the story about the young man who was asked whether he could play the piano? "I don't know," he replied, "I've never tried."

AID NUMBER THREE

Plan your time and schedule of commitments. Provide for continuing satisfactorily with your present responsibilities. Set aside time for proper attention to your efforts toward improvement.

AID NUMBER FOUR

Get reliable information or advice. Seek it from those who *know* and *will tell you* what's best for you.

AID NUMBER FIVE

Read and study all appropriate books, magazines and other publications. Take selected courses at suitable institutions of learning. Strive for intensive absorption rather than extensive superficiality. Try to apply what you learn to your everyday job.

AID NUMBER SIX

Build on the skills you already have and re-shape them into the new ones you need. Remember the old chestnut:

Out-of-towner: Excuse me, Officer. How do I get to Philharmonic Hall?
Policeman: Practice, practice, practice!

AID NUMBER SEVEN

Exercise strong will power over your attitudes. If you can't get rid of an undesirable attitude, at least suppress it. In time it will go away.

AID NUMBER EIGHT

Make yourself conscious of every occasion when you practice an undesirable habit. Force yourself to substitute for it the desired one. While it's *difficult* to break a habit, it's *not impossible* to do so. In time you *can* get *out of* the *old* habit and *into* the *new* one.

AID NUMBER NINE

Continually evaluate the degree of success you've achieved in acquiring the new traits. If at first you don't succeed. . . . When you're reasonably sure you've mastered a particular trait new to you, concentrate on the others. But keep up your periodic, total self-evaluation.

AID NUMBER TEN

Never say: "I can't change." Better to change than to be changed—from a more desirable job to a less desirable one. The human being is highly flexible. You can do well many more things than you may think.

SUCCESS CAPSULE NUMBER TWO

Success Factor Number Two showed you the way to make the most of your present abilities and experience. The discussion was developed along the following lines, proceeding from what you are to what you can easily be:

1. Every management post requires certain specific *K*nowledge, *A*ttitudes, *S*kills and *H*abits. These represent a Manager's *"Kash* assets."

2. You were born with all the attributes you need for successfully meeting your responsibilities: a satisfactory anatomy and physiology, and more than adequate intellectual capacity.

3. Anything else that you may need, in order to improve your job performance, can easily be acquired.

4. Whether you acquire these desired traits is entirely up to you. You build on what you have. The sources of information are readily available. There are people willing and able to help you if you so desire. The rest is up to you.

5. Make an inventory of your own *Kash* and compare it to the *Kash* requirements of your position. Be guided by the checklists provided in this *Success Factor.*

6. The key to self-help is:

- Know what you want and need.
- Find out where it's to be gotten.
- Determine to exert the necessary effort and energy.
- Plan your time.
- Devote as much time to self-improvement as you can possibly spare.
- Try to *apply* what you learn on an everyday basis.
- Continually evaluate yourself and keep on strengthening those areas where you are still weak.
- Be confident that you *can* do it, and you *will* do it.

How You Can
Follow the Best
Road to Profit

This *Success Factor* helps you make the continuing, high-volume profit contribution you owe to your company. You might be able to accomplish this solely because you accept the goal as a management responsibility.

But you're much better off personally—and your chances for profit success are much greater—if you fully agree with and enthusiastically endorse that objective as your *own,* and not the company's alone.

ALWAYS REMEMBER THE COMPANY

Any other approach can be disastrous, as illustrated by the case of a man I know.

He loved his work and came in 'way before anyone else did. He was still at his desk when all the others had gone. He had a sandwich at his work table for lunch, and a thermos of coffee by his side all the time.

A really conscientious executive, would you say? Yes, but for whom and for what?

He was a "one-man organization" within the company. He pursued only those projects which intrigued him. He lived far beyond his budget. He neglected the profitably-productive assignments given to him. And he just wouldn't change.

They finally sent him to work for their strongest competitors!

GET ON THE RIGHT PROFIT ROAD

Your company wants you to make continued, strong contributions to profit. That's really the only reason why they hired you and are retaining you. You *must* follow that road, whether you like it or not.

But the trick is to *like* it.

Look at it this way:

- Your job requires you to meet profit objectives all the time.
- You'll enjoy your work much more if you fully agree with and heartily endorse those objectives.
- You'll do a better job of contributing to such profits if you're enthusiastic about them.
- Your *company's* objectives for you should be entirely consistent with your *own* objectives for yourself.

SET YOUR OWN PROFIT GOALS

You have a profit goal all your own. You're working for a *living,* regardless of whatever other reasons you may have for continuing in your company's employ.

This means that *your* main objective on the job is *your* profit, just as your *company's* main objective—for and through you—is *its* profit.

Be Devoted to Profit

Your best road to profit is one paved with *dedication* to profit and *pleasure in* profit.

You follow that road most successfully when *your* profit goals (for yourself) are consistent with your *company's* profit goals.

Here's how you should regard your *profit* relationships to yourself and to your company:

—I *must* work for a living.

—I might as well do work for which I'm well suited and which I can enjoy.

—That's what my present position offers me.

—My company has employed me only because it feels I can make a significant contribution to their profit.

—I must, therefore, make such a contribution on a continuing basis.

—I might just as well enjoy contributing to my company's profit.

—Besides, the greater my company's profit, the more secure is my own.

—My main personal objective, therefore, is—enthusiastically—to help my company continue to meet its main objective: *profit.*

SEE PROFIT AS YOUR COMPANY SEES IT

You must pursue profit for your company with the exact "frame of reference" *it* employs. Your company wants you to plan, speak and act at all times in such a way that you, and your subordinates, constantly contribute to *this* kind of profit:
- The greatest possible at this time.
- Consistent with other company goals.
- Increasing all the time.

Avoid Substitutes

The word *profits* is sometimes replaced, in company publications and outside communications media, by other terms. These are appropriate to those channels of expression.

But *you* must think, talk and act *profit.* This word has a significance and an impact which no other concept can equal, especially when it comes to your subordinates.

An Example

I came across a situation in a client company which illustrates what I'm emphasizing here.

Sam Revere, the Chief Engineer of an electronics company, insisted on speaking of his company's *earnings,* because that was the term used on their annual report. His boss and I both agreed that Sam was thenceforth to think and express himself in terms of *profit,* since this was a word which his subordinates—all the way down the line—understood clearly and precisely.

Interestingly enough, Sam's preference for the word *earnings* turned out to reflect a real attitude on his part *against* having company profit as his own personal goal. Fortunately, his attitude was ultimately straightened out.

ANALYZE THE ELEMENTS OF PROFIT

You can make the proper contribution to profit only if you:
- Really want to.
- Know what elements go into creating profit.

Let's see what these elements are.

BALANCE COST WITH PRODUCTIVITY

You are responsible for two major profit factors:
1. The Company *facilities* entrusted to you.
2. The kind of *productivity* you can turn out.

Let's analyze each of these elements.

Optimize Your Cost Center

You're a company "cost center." You have been charged with using carefully and wisely some of your company's assets, selected from the following list:
- Real property.
- Fixtures and furniture.
- Machinery and equipment.
- Utilities.
- Parts and tools.
- Materials and supplies.
- Employees (including yourself).
- Finished products.
- Money in whatever form.
- Company reputation.

Be Cost-Conscious

You are "costing" your company "money" if:
—You fail to use any assets that you're supposed to; or
—You use improperly those you're charged with.

Use Assets Wisely

Your first contribution to company profit, then, is to make sure that you and *all* your subordinates constantly:
1. Use all company assets assigned to you.
2. Use no assets not under your responsibility.
3. Make the most economical, efficient and effective use of those assets which you are responsible for.

Get on Top of Costs

Your first contribution to company profit is to fashion a Cost Center —out of yourself and your people—which makes maximum/optimum use of assets assigned to you *at the lowest possible cost* to your company.

MAXIMIZE YOUR PRODUCTIVITY

Your second profit responsibility is to put your efficiently-run Cost Center to maximum/optimum productive use. This means that you will:

- Adhere strictly to standards set *for* you and (properly) *by* you.
- Get maximum/optimum use of the assets you employ.
- Be constantly conscious of the need to "spend" the smallest amount possible of company "money" (assets) consistent with maximum/optimum desired productivity.

ESTABLISH SUITABLE NON-MONETARY GOALS

You will agree that if your company continued to operate too long without satisfactory profits, it would be well on the way to closing its doors. You can't indefinitely buy thousands of dresses at fifteen dollars apiece, sell them for fourteen dollars apiece, and hope to make up for the loss by the volume of dresses you sell.

Adopt One Set of Goals

As long as your company has maximum/optimum profits on a continuing basis, it does have certain additional goals. You must make these *company* goals *your own* also.

Naturally, these non-monetary aims are valid only if:

- The results of your and your company's pursuit of those other goals is consistent with the prime objective of *profit*.
- You try, wherever possible, to turn even the pursuit of those *other* goals into resulting company profit.

ADOPT THESE OBJECTIVES

1. Reputation

To establish and maintain throughout the country the best possible company reputation for quality, courtesy, service and growth.

Of course, such a reputation inevitably leads to greater profits, and there's nothing wrong with that. But you and your company want to feel genuinely proud of the reception you get from the public at large, and from your customers in particular.

You want this above and beyond profit, but *not without* profit.

PORTRAIT NUMBER ONE: Alex Piser is in charge of personnel recruitment for a large, nationally-known food manufacturer.

He has told me that whenever a preliminary interview with a job candidate reveals the latter's complete inadequacy for any work there, he spends a little more time with the applicant than really necessary. Not enough to prevent Alex from meeting all his other obligations, but just enough to send away a man who likes the company.

"This fellow," said Alex, "will go into a supermarket on Saturday with his wife. When she reaches for a box of our foods from the shelf, I don't want him to tell her not to buy my company's product because I was rude to him."

2. Service

To serve our country and its various communities.

I'm talking here of conscious, positive activities which you and your company engage in, where profit is not your *main* goal. Of course, you won't spend more time or money on such activities than your company feels it can afford. But look at it this way:

- Your company is part of this country's socio-economic life, and a member of one or more of the nation's local communities.
- Your company owes it to our worthwhile institutions to participate in their vital activities.

Your company's cooperation with them will not only repay somewhat its debt to a country which makes success possible; such cooperation will necessarily give your company greater acceptance as a reputable organization within the community.

PARTICIPATE IN COMMUNITY LIFE

Here is a partial list of suggestions on how you can participate suitably in community life on your own and your company's behalf:

- membership on the local Board of Education.
- occasional offers of company facilities for meetings of worthwhile community organizations.
- attendance at church affairs.
- cooperation with government commissions or committees.
- membership in local service clubs.
- well-considered financial contributions to worthy causes.

PORTRAIT NUMBER TWO: Hugh Allison was the Public Relations Director of his company. Headquarters was in a town of some 200,000 people, and they had branches in a dozen other towns of comparable size throughout the country.

Hugh drew up and submitted to his boss a plan for continuing participation in community activities. In every one of their localities three or four executives were designated to participate in specific community activities. They did this as individuals, but it was widely known that they worked for that company.

In addition, each location had one man in charge of making company contributions to local fund-raising drives.

And nationally, Hugh saw to it that there was always some company executive functioning on a Presidential committee or as a trustee on some semi-autonomous governmental institution.

3. Employee Well-Being

To provide all company employees with the best possible opportunity to enjoy and benefit from their work.

You will, of course, not permit the pursuit of this goal to cut down on the achievement of profit objectives. But as long as you continue to strive for maximum profit, there's every reason why you should also want to help your people derive the greatest satisfaction and benefits from their work with you.

Naturally, there are some people who simply won't or can't be satisfied, no matter what you do for them. But they're in the minority.

Elements Involved

You'll easily accomplish your *satisfaction* objective if you just put your mind and energy to it.

- Continue to contribute satisfactorily to company profit.
- Keep employees (management and non-management alike) contented with their work.
- Be considerate of their well-being.
- Offer them every reasonable opportunity to develop and grow with the company.

Your Motivation

Why should you want to do all this? Because your company's employees are part of this country's population and deserve the greatest possible opportunity for a good life as long as they're willing to do their expected share.

And, of course, you will inevitably get better and more productivity out of them if you treat them right. This leads right to greater profit for your company and you.

PORTRAIT NUMBER THREE: Ben Cooper was Traffic Manager for his company. He had seven Regional Managers working for him, and each one of them had a number of Dispatchers under *him.*

Ben set very high performance standards for his immediate subordinates, and saw to it that they consistently lived up to his expectations. But Ben was genuinely interested in his people.

Whenever possible he gave his Regional Managers a choice of location. He consulted them a year in advance on their vacation-time preferences. He visited each one of them at least five times a year. And when he did, he took the Manager and his wife out to dinner in a very fine restaurant.

Ben's men worked hard for him, and consistently met company profit goals. And they liked him and the company.

Did Ben act this way only because he knew that he'd get better results from it? Not Ben. He really liked people and respected their right to the good life.

And so long as they did what they were supposed to, he was ready to help make them happier.

What if this also helped to make them do a better job for Ben?

4. Managerial Pleasure

To derive the highest possible satisfaction from doing well the kind of work you like to do.

If a management man is working for his present company only because he can't get a better job anywhere else, I suggest he do one of two things:

- Get a job with another company where he *can* enjoy his work more, *or* . . .
- Find elements in his present job which he *can* enjoy, and work hard at eventually making the number of those elements co-extensive with his whole job.

PUT PROFIT ABOVE PLEASURE

Even if you don't enjoy your work, or part of it, you're still going to have to make the kind of profit contribution that's expected of you. So why not enjoy it? You can always find ways of liking what you have to do.

An old musical comedy had a solo song whose theme was: If I can't have the girl I love, I'll love the girl I have.

FIND PLEASURE IN PROFIT

It's a perfectly justifiable objective for the people in a company to want to derive great satisfaction from their work—as long as this doesn't interfere with profits. Company presidents feel this way. So do the various vice presidents.

A man who enjoys his work will generally do it better. And, conversely, if he does it better, he enjoys it more.

PORTRAIT NUMBER FOUR: Arnold Pratt had been Assistant Plant Manager in an aerospace company, and had liked his job very much. What gave him the greatest confidence, perhaps, was the fact that he could always consult the Plant Manager when in doubt on decisions.

Arnold was transferred to the position of Program Manager for a new government contract. Being conscientious and loyal he did his best to meet his new responsibilities successfully. And he did this to the entire satisfaction of his new boss.

There was only one thing that bothered Arnold about the new job: the customer—the government—looked to him directly for decisions on day-to-day problems. There just wasn't any opportunity for Arnold to delay action so he could consult his immediate superior. Arnold was not enjoying his work.

He told this to his boss, who pointed out the following:

- The new job was an important step in Arnold's continuing advancement in the company.
- It was good training for Arnold's eventual assumption of positions with even greater decision-making requirements.
- No man can continue to hold a high-level management position without making important decisions by himself.
- If decision-making was "inevitable," he might just as well "relax and enjoy it."

Arnold found, after a while, that his boss was right. Today he not only *makes* most of his own decisions; he *enjoys* making them.

SUCCESS CAPSULE NUMBER THREE

This *Success Factor* pointed out the importance to you and your company of having, following and achieving the proper objectives in your job. Here are the highlights:

  1. You must make every justifiable *company* objective also *your own* objective. What's good enough for them is good enough for you. Besides, your company is going to continue to have those objec-

tives, so you might as well make them your own if you're to keep on being successful and happy in your work.

2. *Profit* is the most important single objective of your company. Your goal on the job, therefore, must be constantly to make the greatest contribution you can to your company's profit.

3. Your contribution to profit comes partly from intelligent cost control and partly from seeing to it that you and your people consistently produce to your and their greatest and best ability along expected lines.

4. Your company seeks, in addition to the profit objective—and consistent with it—the continual achievement of the following *supplemental goals:*

   a. Company reputation for quality, courtesy, service and growth.

   b. Service to the country and to the company's various communities.

   c. A genuine interest in the well-being of all its employees.

   d. Personal satisfaction for all in working for and with the company to the best of their abilities.

5. You must make these supplemental objectives your own, too. They not only help you contribute maximally and optimally to your company's profit, but also give you greater personal pleasure in being associated with such an enterprise.

How You Can Turn Paper Work into Paper Money

This *Success Factor* tackles the ever-present problem faced by management people: how to attend to necessary paper work while concentrating on profitable productivity and cost control. You, as a management man, *must* solve this problem.

An Example

Take this case, which illustrates the kind of situation I'm talking about:

Matt Atkins was Superintendent of Manufacturing in a paper mill. He had three foremen reporting to him, in addition to an Industrial Engineer, a Quality Control Manager and a Chief Inspector.

Matt was a true management man. He believed in frequent face-to-face communications and supervision, and was generally to be found among his men in the various departments.

The only trouble was that Matt was responsible, also, for certain records and reports. He complained to me that if he was to keep up with his paper work, he'd have to spend less time where he felt he was most needed: where the production was going on.

I soon found out why Matt was having a problem. His office was poorly organized. He had no paper work system. It took him twice as long to keep records and make reports as it would have if he'd done better planning for this important responsibility of his.

51

I helped him set up the kind of paper work organization and procedures which I describe in this *Success Factor*.

Matt is a changed man today. He's still out on the floor as much as he should be. But he gets his paper work done too: promptly, efficiently and effectively. *And* he actually enjoys taking care of it.

ANALYZE YOUR PRESENT PAPER WORK HABITS

Before you start to plan improvements in your paper work setup and procedures, make a careful analysis of how you are *now* handling this responsibility.

Recall Your Recent Experiences

Think back to your last few weeks on the job. Did you periodically find yourself unable to devote the necessary amount of time and attention to the people around you because your nose was stuck in paper work? Did it really have to take all the time it did? Were you properly organized for it?

Examine Your Present Practices

Try this experiment for a week:

Every time you sit down at your desk to work by yourself, fill in the blanks on a form similar to the accompanying one.

At the end of the week total up the time you've spent on desk work. Compare it with the total time you've spent that week with other people, or away from your desk on company business.

Analyze Your Time Allotment

If your comparison shows a disproportion in favor of paper work, you *must* establish the proper balance between it and your inter-personal responsibilities. You are then in need of the kind of system which follows.

ADOPT A "PRO-SYSTEMATIC" ATTITUDE

Before you can accept and follow the paper work procedure I'm going to suggest to you, you'll first have to:

- Create an attitude of self-discipline in the handling of paper work.
- Overcome any indifference you may have to orderliness.
- Be ready to change those of your present habits which interfere with paper work efficiency.

I stress *changed attitudes* because my experience has convinced me that this is a necessary first step.

Date	Began at	A.M.	P.M.	Ended at	A.M.	P.M.	Nature of work

A Case in Point

It happened in a publishing house for which I did a month's consulting work.

I'd been given a small office across the hall from Mac Roper, one of their editors. Mac and I had hit it off well from the start, and he'd often drop in to chat with me. Occasionally he'd kid me because I kept my desk top so orderly all the time. One day he invited me into his office, and, showing me the six inches of littered papers on his desk top, boasted, "See how untidy my desk is? Yet, I can find anything on it whenever I want to."

One Tuesday, shortly after that day, I'd been expecting a rather important memo. When it hadn't arrived by Thursday, I went after it myself and was told that it had been sent to me on time. Of course, I was given a copy right away.

On Friday Mac came walking into my office with a sheet of paper in his hand.

"Bill, this memo seems to be for you."

"Why, Mac, that's the one I've been looking for all week. How come you've got it now?"

"Well, I was looking for a letter on my desk top, today, and—just as I'd told you I could—I found it at once, three or four layers down. I just happened to notice that this memo was right under that letter. Someone must have put it on my desk by mistake, and then it got snowed under by papers that were put down on top of it."

Be Master of Your Paper Work

Your goal should be: *effective* and *efficient personal organization.* The key to this is to be able to find a piece of paper, a magazine, a book or any other document *at the precise moment* when you need it.

Of course, if you have an efficient secretary this is no problem—you simply ask her to get it and bring it to you. But if you're like the management men I've worked with, you're in *personal* control of many documents which you must refer to, which you'd like to be able to find exactly when you want them—and can't.

MAKE YOUR "OFFICE" CONTRIBUTE TO PROFIT

Whatever room or space you use as an "office," you should make it *work for you* efficiently. Before you can bring this about, you must take the time to organize or re-organize it. You may have to stay after hours once to do this, or come in *one* Saturday. But it's well worth the trouble.

Remember, though, that once you rearrange things properly, you'd better stick to the rules all the time, or you'll soon be right back where you started.

Categorize Your Papers

Your first step toward achieving office efficiency is: Divide all your papers and other documents into these two classifications:

1. *The passive group:* those items to which you may want to refer from time to time, but which you don't have to remember or bring up at any specific time. For example: a technical manual, the file on your company's R and D reports, drawings you may need to look at again some day, your company's policy manual.

2. *The active group:* papers representing things you have to remember to take care of at specific times. (I'll give examples of these later on in this *Success Factor.*)

Optimize Your Office Facilities

Your next step is to make sure that your office is set up for maximum efficiency. I suggest an arrangement like the one in Diagram 1, and will refer to the diagram as I go along.

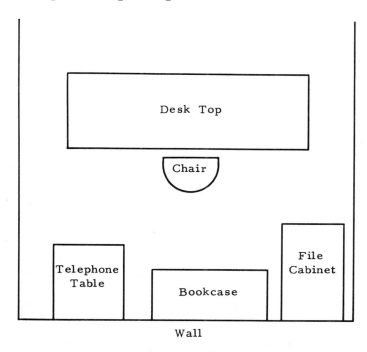

Diagram 1

Store Passive Documents Efficiently

Your first requirement, here, is to keep only those items which you *really* need or *probably will* need. In this connection, let me re-tell this old story.

The place is the huge library in the newly-built mansion of the newly-rich tycoon. The cast of characters: the tycoon and the minister of his church.

They have just finished dinner and the minister is examining some of the hundreds of handsomely-bound sets of newly-bought books on the shelves. He discovers that the pages have not been cut in any of the books.
The dialogue:

> *The Minister:* I see that you have many books.
> *The Tycoon:* Oh, yes. Books are my friends.
> *The Minister:* So that's why you don't cut them!

Discard Useless Papers

Don't clutter up your office with books and documents that aren't and won't be needed there. Either send them to central files or throw them into "File Thirteen."

Inform Your Secretary

Make sure that your secretary knows and understands the system you're using for the greater efficiency of your office. And extend this knowledge to any others who may have access to it. Impress on them the way that you want your documents kept—in the way that you've explained to them—*all the time.*

Put Documents Where You Can Find Them

Here is how you can most efficiently arrange those books and documents which you do need, or can profitably use, in your office:

- Keep as close to your desk as possible those documents to which you may have to refer frequently.
- Keep all *books* in *one* place, all *magazines* in *another,* all *newspapers together, maps* and *drawings in suitable containers, loose papers in file folders* (and those in drawers or cabinets), etc.
- Except for books and other bulky items which you need to refer to very often, follow the principle of alphabetical arrangement (by title, topic, author, etc., depending on what's most useful to you).

Put Things Back Where They Belong

One final caution in respect to your passive documents: When you remove one of them from where it was, be sure to return it to that same place when you're finished with it.

KEEP OFFICE FACILITIES NEAT AND ORDERLY

You'll get greater efficiency out of your office furniture if you use it somewhat like this:

Make Desk Drawers Work for You

Keep in the drawers of your desk only those supplies which you need on a regular basis: letterheads, envelopes, carbon paper, bond paper and second sheets, pads, clips, elastics, pencils, pens, forms, rulers and similar implements, stapler and its supplies, 3-hole punch, index cards, stamps, file of addresses, Scotch tape, checkbooks, etc. Use compartments or little boxes where appropriate.

And: keep those items handiest which you use most frequently. Get into the habit of putting the same kinds of things always in the same place. The trick is to be able to find whatever you want at the precise moment that you want it.

If one of your desk drawers is made for files, arrange and use it as described later, for file cabinets.

Capitalize on Your Telephone Table

You'll get maximum efficiency from your use of the telephone if you'll set up its table like this:

- On the top keep your telephone(s), dictating machine, intercom, etc., arranged for easy access and most frequent use. (Wires and other equipment, intertwined or tangled, can cut down on efficiency.)
- Have a fixed pad and pencil right on the table top, so placed that you can easily make notes with one hand as you use a piece of equipment with the other.

Profit from Your Bookcase

Keep in your bookcase only those books, magazines, newspapers, manuals, drawings, etc., which you constantly or frequently need to refer to. Include your most-frequently required telephone and other directories.

Arrange the contents of the case by type of document, by size and by topic.

Place your books and other materials in such a way that you can put your hand on what you want within seconds of your need for it. It's better not to have to move one book in order to get at another.

Control Your File Cabinet

Keep in your files only those papers you may have to refer to quickly or frequently. A simple alphabetical system is the best.

Be sure you know where your secretary puts papers she's authorized to file for you.

MAKE YOUR MEMORY "AUTOMATIC"

Your job inevitably requires you to take the initiative on a wide variety of activities. For these, you can't wait until someone else cues you to action. Either *you* remember to do what you're supposed to or you don't do it—at all, or on time.

With so many things to take care of, you don't want to be trying constantly to recall the next item you have to take care of. Nor do you want to keep on worrying about what you might have forgotten to do.

Remember to Do What You Must

Before I suggest to you a method for making your memory "automatic," let's review some of the areas of your responsibility where such a device can be helpful.

Here are *Nine Remembering Requirements* which you must continually and successfully meet:

1. To be sure to take care of all the activities which require your initiative: promptly, correctly and completely.
2. To keep all appointments and meet all commitments and deadlines: on time, accurately and thoroughly.
3. To be sure to check up on matters which you've delegated, assigned or left to others; before it's too late, and in necessary detail.
4. To make sure to plan steps to be taken in the immediate or long-range future: well enough in advance to make possible a bang-up job.
5. To be sure to do everything you promised or were supposed to do: exactly *when* and *how* expected.
6. To make certain that you prepare, send out and/or receive reports: when due, and in proper shape.

7. To be able to do all of this without wasting time trying to remember, or find things connected with, steps requiring your initiative.
8. To be able to tell at a moment's glance whether you can put aside Task A, and for how long, in order to undertake Task B, which has just come up.
9. To have complete peace of mind in all of this because your "remembering" system is "automatic."

Use a Tickler System

Your first step in achieving "automatic" memory is to set up and properly use an efficient, effective tickler system. Here's how I suggest you do this:

Set aside a section of a readily-handy file drawer for your tickler file. Have your secretary prepare for you 45 file folders in the accompanying manner:

Number of Folders	*Tabbed as follows*
one	"Every Day"
thirty-one	1, 2, 3, . . . 31
twelve	with a month of the year, in sequence, from January through December
one	"Next Year's"

Put these folders into the tickler drawer in the above order.

Put Active Papers into the Tickler

Whenever you want to remember to pay attention, at some time in the future, to a particular piece of paper, put it into its appropriate tickler folder. Here are your guidelines for this kind of sorting:

If you want to refer to that paper again	*Put it into the folder tabbed*
Every day, until you know what final disposition to make of it	"Every Day"
On a specific day of the current month	with the number of that day
Some time in any of the following months	with the name of the month desired
Some time in the next year (or following years)	"Next Year's"

If you think you may want to find a particular paper (destined for your tickler) some time before it "comes up" in normal tickler sequence, put a copy of your tickler note in your alphabetical passive files, with an indication of where the original is to be found in the tickler.

Have Your Tickler Remember for You

A suggested technique for using your tickler is presented below. If you'll get into the habit of following this procedure regularly, your "memory" (of things you have to attend to in the future) will become "automatic."

1. Consult your tickler according to the following schedule:
   a. Preferably, every evening before you leave the office, planning for the next day.
   b. If that's not possible, the very first thing before you start your work, preparing for that same day.
   c. Before you go on a trip which will keep you away from your office for one or more days, anticipating that day or those days.

2. Whenever you consult your tickler according to schedule, look in the folders, indicated just below, and put all papers you extract in one pile: for sorting, as discussed in 3., below.
   a. Look first in the "Every Day" Folder to see whether you want to take anything out at that time.
   b. Then look in the folder(s) for the day(s) being planned for, and extract all papers from it (them).
      1) If you're planning for the last day of any one month, empty out, also, all the papers for the *following* month.
      2) If you're planning for December 31st, empty out, also, all the papers in the "Next Year's" Folder.

3. Now sort all the papers (which you've extracted from the folders) and dispose of them in one of the following ways, whichever is appropriate.
   a. Put them in your desk "Sort Box" (described further on in this chapter).
   b. Put them in your "To Be Filed" tray (also described later in the chapter).
   c. Put them into another tickler folder or (other tickler folders) for future reference. (This is especially applicable to papers extracted from a folder for the following month or from the "Next Year's" Folder. For example, papers extracted on March 31st from the April Folder may now have to be re-distributed in the numbered folders, since April now becomes the

current month. And papers extracted on December 31st from the "Next Year's" Folder may have to be re-distributed in the folders for the various months of the new current year.)

    d. Discard them if no longer needed.

MAKE YOUR DESK TOP WORK FOR YOU

You can easily cut 50% from the time you need for your paper work if you'll set up and maintain a continuingly-orderly desk top.

I suggest an arrangement similar to that depicted in Diagram 2. (Explanations of the items shown are given in the text.)

Desk Top

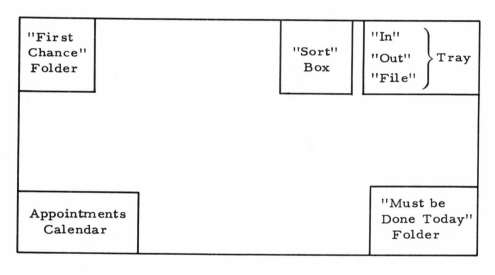

Diagram 2

Profit from Your Desk Top

Here are some suggestions for keeping your desk top continually efficient, and for deriving maximum benefit from it:

1. *Incoming papers.*

Instruct your secretary (and all others who have authority to bring papers and other documents to your attention) always to put things into your "In" tray, *and nowhere else*. The only exception should be that if you're out, when they deliver a very important paper requiring your immediate attention, they can put it squarely in the front center of your desk (*not* on top of anything already there), properly weighted down so it won't blow away.

2. *Notes away from your desk.*

Wherever you are, away from your desk, make a note of important matters you'll want to take care of when you get back to it. Always carry a small pad and pencil with you. If you put the note into your pocket, make it the same pocket all the time.

3. *First steps in the office.*

Just as soon as possible after you come into your office, follow as much of this routine as is applicable.

    a. Empty the contents of your memo pocket and your brief case into the Sort Box.

    b. Look to see whether there are any important papers which have been placed on the front center of your desk top, and dispose of them properly at once.

    c. Consult the other items on your desk top, as indicated in 5., following.

4. *Miscellaneous papers.*

Never put a piece of paper or other document *down* just because you don't know what else to do with it at that moment. Put it into your Sort Box.

5. *Tackling the desk top.*

Every time you begin to attack a portion of your day's paper work:

    a. Look, first, at your Appointment Calendar. This should be reserved for only *fixed* appointments (for visits or phone calls) for specific days and times. Don't use it for any other kinds of memos.

    b. Make mental note (or set your alarm, if necessary, keeping the clock on your telephone table top) of the next fixed appointment.

    c. Next, consult your "Must Be Done Today" Folder.

        1) In it should be kept only those papers which represent work you *must* do today, in descending order of chronological requirements.

2) You can, of course, shift papers from one folder to another as changes in plan require.

3) Before taking on the papers in the "Must Be Done Today" Folder, you can always judge, just by looking at the top one, whether you must tackle it at once or can postpone it. If the latter, make a mental note (or set your alarm) for when you *must* come back to it.

4) If, while you're doing a particular piece of paper work, someone asks to take up some of your time, you need only consult your Appointment Calendar and the top paper in your "Must Be Done Today" Folder, to know whether you can give him any time, and, if so, how much.

d. Make it your business to find time, as often as possible during the day, to go through your Sort Box. From it put papers and documents into your tickler, into any of the trays or folders on your desk top or into the waste basket.

e. If you do your own filing, be sure to take care of it as frequently as possible. The same goes for your secretary if she's in charge of that duty.

f. You might occasionally check to make sure that your Out Box is cleared as often as it should be.

g. Whenever you've nothing else to do, or can spare the time, go to your "First Chance" Folder. This, too, should have its contents arranged in descending order of chronological importance. This might be one of the folders you want to take with you for the evening (or weekend) or on a trip. But be sure to bring it back to the office on the next business day.

6. *Preparing for the next day.*

Before you leave the office at the end of the day, take care of *all* of the following matters:

a. Tear off (or turn down) the current page of your Appointment Calendar.

b. Check the "First Chance" Folder to see whether there's anything on the top, and just below the top, which should be transferred to another place.

c. Clear your Sort Box.

d. Check your whole tray for proper emptying.

e. Be sure there's nothing at the top of your "Must Be Done

Today" Folder which hasn't been done today, or transferred to a more appropriate place in your system.

f. Check your tickler file for the next business day(s).
g. Make sure there's nothing lying about on your desk top outside of the appropriate containers. Don't do what my friend Jack Barnes used to. He cleared his desk top every afternoon by shoving all of its contents into a desk drawer, only to be dumped on his desk top again the next day.
h. Be sure you haven't left anything out which is confidential, but make a note (in the appropriate place) that you've put it wherever you did.
i. Make sure that everything is properly weighted down which might otherwise blow away.
j. Note the time of your first appointment the next business day.
k. Leave the office with your mind at ease that everything you've left behind can really wait until you come back.

7. *Paper work away from your desk.*

If you take papers away from the office for homework, or on a trip, set up a system in your attaché case. Use folders and tabs which resemble pertinent portions of your desk system. Keep your ambulatory arrangements orderly. Then, when you get back, it's that much easier to sort papers from your case to your office.

Folders like the following will be helpful:

- Tickler for trip (one folder, with papers arranged in chronological sequence, a date notation appearing on the top corner of each paper).
- Ambulatory date book (for use only away from the office and carefully synchronized with what's on your Appointment Calendar for those days).
- "First Chance" Folder.
- "Sort" Folder.
- "For Out Tray" Folder.
- "For File Tray" Folder.
- "Must Be Done Today" Folder.

SUCCESS CAPSULE NUMBER FOUR

In this *Success Factor* I've suggested a practical system for making your paper work more efficient and more effective in your pursuit of company profit.

1. Make an assessment of your present approach to paper work, to see where you can make helpful changes.
2. Adopt an attitude of self-discipline and orderliness toward your paper-work obligations.
3. Treat all papers from the standpoint of whether they require *active* attention or are merely for *passive* reference.
4. Organize your office facilities in a way which will lead to more efficient and effective handling of your paper work.
5. Keep your office facilities orderly at all times, as an aid to efficient paper-work activities.
6. Make your memory "automatic" through the use of a set of efficient habits in storing and recalling papers and other documents.
7. Adopt and practice continuing habits of efficient office work and procedures.

Maximize Your Managerial Relationships

How to
Work Effectively
with Your Boss

This *Success Factor* deals with how you can increase and improve your contribution to your company's profit (*and* yours) by establishing and maintaining the most effective relationship possible with your immediate superior.

MEET YOUR BOSS MORE THAN HALF-WAY

Your main responsibility to your company is to carry out—continuously, profitably and willingly—your immediate superior's orders, instructions or wishes.

In the first instance it is, of course, *his* duty to let you know what he expects of you. And he must motivate you to do it in the most effective and efficient way possible.

Anticipate His Wishes

But if he should be slow or remiss in meeting *his* obligation, you're not necessarily off the hook. He may *still* feel or say, justifiably or not, that you *should* have done what he wanted, the way he wanted it. And this, even if he didn't spell it out for you. He'd be perfectly justified in telling you that you as a manager should have known what he wanted.

69

Value the Boss

Furthermore, whether or not you agree with him on this, he's still your boss. And he's going to keep on being your boss. So, you'd better meet him more than half-way, if you want to:

- Continue to work for him.
- Make the best possible contribution to company profit.
- Maintain a solid reputation for managerial excellence.
- Have peace of mind on the job.

You can easily accomplish all this by carefully and consistently following these *Six Golden Rules* for working effectively with the boss:

1. Find out what he expects of you.
2. Find out how to do this successfully.
3. Line up your "profit tools."
4. Make your own decisions.
5. Make yourself available to your boss.
6. Treat your boss right.

Have the Proper Attitude

There's a good reason why I emphasize your responsibility to meet your boss more than half-way. I'd like to make sure you won't feel, express or act on sentiments like some I've heard from managers:

"Why should I worry if my boss goofs? That's *his* problem."

"It's no skin off *my* nose. I'm only his assistant. *He's* getting more money than *I* am."

"If that's the way he wanted it, why didn't he tell me? Am I supposed to be a mind-reader or something?"

FIND OUT WHAT HE EXPECTS OF YOU

The first step in your campaign to meet your boss more than half-way is to find out *exactly* what he wants you to do. And go after this if *he* fails to take the initiative to let you know it.

Follow These Three Sure-Fire Steps

1. Keep your eyes and ears open for any new or different activities which might affect you and your responsibility.

2. Estimate your possible participation in the job: the *what* and the *when*.

3. If you don't hear from your boss about it by the time you think you should have, ask him whether you were right in your assumption that he'd be requiring you to undertake the assignment in question.

Don't Pass the Buck

You gain nothing, and can lose much, by shrugging off this last-mentioned responsibility.

Don't do what Morris Winters did in a containerization plant.

The President had told him that a group of prospective customers would come through the next day to inspect the latest hydraulic-loading equipment Morris's people had just assembled. Morris had everything ready for the visit except a container to be lifted on to the trailer. After the visitors had gone, the President expressed his disappointment in Morris. Winters replied that the President hadn't told him to have a container ready.

Be Tactful

When you ask your immediate superior about instructions or orders which *he* should have initiated, you'll want to make sure he doesn't get any false impressions.

Don't let him think you're trying to show him up as negligent or remiss. You'll therefore want to express yourself as subtly and as tactfully as possible.

Here are some samples of the kinds of statements you might make:

1. "Pat, I'm all caught up with my work, and thought I'd anticipate you a little. Want to tell me now what the next job is, so I can have more time to plan it?"

2. "Pat, my men are finishing up on the units you assigned to me last week. Anything else you'd like to give me now that I can have them do as soon as they're through?"

FIND OUT HOW TO DO SUCCESSFULLY WHAT HE EXPECTS

If your boss asks you to undertake a job that you don't know how to do satisfactorily, either:

- Figure out by yourself how to lick it.
- Ask someone else whom you can quite properly approach.
- Tell your boss that you'd appreciate his advice or help on it.

Be a Prime Mover

Here, again, if the man upstairs neglects to show you *how* to do something, you're not really expected to know, take the initiative to find out. And if you can get the necessary information without taking up his time, so much the better. But if that's the only or most efficient route to follow, you lose nothing by asking him about it directly.

Be Willing to Admit Your Shortcomings

There's nothing wrong in not knowing how to do one or two of the things you're asked to take care of. And if you try to cover up for an excusable lack of knowledge, you're bound to get into trouble.

An Example

Take the case of Jim Fell. He was Contracts Negotiator for his division of the company. There was a Corporate Contracts Negotiator, too, available to all divisions for guidance and help.

Jim was jealous of the corporate negotiator.

On one occasion Jim was seated at the negotiation table with a customer for his division's products. The customer's negotiator proposed a clause which was entirely new to Jim. He'd had no experience with the subject-matter involved. He knew that he could have temporized in the negotiations until he could contact the corporate negotiator for advice. But his unwillingness to show inferior know-how got the better of him. He went ahead on the new clause on his own.

When the proposed contract came up to the corporate level for review, the company had to reject the clause in question. It was entirely at variance with their policy. It had to be renegotiated, with much loss of face and time-money.

Seek the Help of Others

When you don't know how to do something well, ask someone who does. You lose no stature from this. *And,* you get the job done right.

An Illustration

Take, for example, the case of John McGee.

He was asked to have swatch books prepared for the company's new product line, upholstered furniture. He'd never before put such volumes together, even though he'd been Advertising Manager for many years. Up to that time his work had been exclusively with case goods.

His boss, the Marketing Director, had just taken it for granted that John would know how to fill the new assignment. John went to the newly-named Upholstered Furniture Product Manager. Between the two of them they turned out a real professional swatch book.

LINE UP YOUR "PROFIT TOOLS"

Now you know what your boss wants you to do, and are thoroughly informed on how to do it successfully. Your next responsibility is to make sure *at once* that you have, or get, all the facilities you'll need to do the job properly.

Conserve Your Company's Assets

A Cost Control Supervisor once complained to me about some of the managers in his company. They would accept assignments from the boss without checking whether sufficient provision had been made for the necessary equipment or tools. Then, when they'd already parceled the work out to their men, they'd suddenly discover they didn't have all the things needed to do the job satisfactorily.

While the manager scrounged around to find or get what was missing, there was down-time on machines. And workers were idle. The only thing that went on uninterruptedly was the accumulation of hours for which the men would have to be paid.

Consult the Checklist

Here are the kinds of facilities you might need to complete the tasks delegated to you:
- Machinery
- Equipment
- Space
- Materials
- Manpower
- Supplies
- Utilities
- Tools
- Parts
- Manuals

Go After What You Need

If your analysis reveals that you don't have enough of the right kinds of facilities for the job in question, either:

—Get them from an appropriate source other than your boss; or

—Take the initiative to ask him for what you need. Here, too, tact may be essential so that he won't think you're being critical of him.

MAKE YOUR OWN DECISIONS

Suppose your boss doesn't spell everything out for you in great detail. Or, what if something comes up during the work which neither of you anticipated?

You're of greater help to him if you make your own decisions and solve your own problems.

Avoid Petty Questions

In this connection, the story is told of the new reporter on a metropolitan newspaper. His City Editor had asked him to cover a particular arrest at Police Headquarters.

The cub inquired of the Editor:

"How do I get to Police Headquarters, sir?"

He never got there. While he was writing obituaries, an older newspaperman, who had overheard the conversation, tipped him off:

"You never ask a City Editor to help you solve a problem as simple as how to get to the place of an assignment."

Have Confidence in Your Own Judgment

When you are faced with two or more alternatives, analyze them carefully. Weigh the consequences of one against those of the other. If you're reasonably sure your choice is sound, act on it. Failure to do so can slow you down, as well as lose you the respect of your superiors.

A Case in Point

A good example of the undesirable results of indecisiveness comes from an aircraft manufacturing company.

Henry Fowler was the Chief Design Engineer. He sat in on all top-level production-planning meetings. He had every opportunity to ask questions of the other department heads.

Yet, every time the Vice President of Manufacturing approved

Henry's designs, Henry felt he had to take one additional step. He insisted on going to his boss for an OK on the drawings and plans. There was nothing wrong with them.

His superior repeatedly asked Henry not to consult him so frequently. But Henry kept right on, always finding some excuse for going there.

The work was considerably slowed down by Henry's inability to deliver final designs on time. And he was passed over when the next vacancy occurred for promotion to a higher position.

Take the Bull by the Horns

Here are *Nine Steps* you should take in arriving at a good decision or a wise solution to a problem:

1. Tackle the decision or problem just as soon as it presents itself to you.

2. Marshal all available facts and accumulate pertinent opinions.

3. Think of the various alternatives open to you in the light of those facts or opinions.

4. Write each alternative down on a sheet of paper. Under each alternative set down the reasons why you think it's a good one. Put in, also, any disadvantages you see in acting on those reasons. You'll find the format on page 76 helpful in taking this step.

5. Compare the various alternatives with each other and select the one which you think has the most advantages and the fewest disadvantages.

6. If you're *really* not sure whether you ought to make the decision yourself, or solve the problem on your own:

    a. Come to an interim conclusion on the alternative you'd select.

    b. Go to your boss and tell him what the situation is, what you've done to arrive at a satisfactory resolution, and what you think should be done.

    c. Explain why you felt you wanted his opinion this time, and ask him whether he agrees with your analysis.

7. Put the final decision or solution into effect as soon as you've arrived at it. Let everyone involved know at once—and accurately—exactly what you've decided. Even if your superior helped you arrive at your decision or solution, communicate it as your own.

8. Just as soon as possible after the decision becomes effective, watch the related situation very closely and carefully. If you discover that you were wrong in your decision, or made a poor choice:

    a. Put a stop to its execution.

    b. Tell all concerned that you want to re-examine the problem.

Alternative	
Reasons why it might be a good alternative	*Disadvantages in acting on those reasons*

    c. And do so promptly, following as many of the above steps as necessary.

    d. Communicate the new or revised decision or solution promptly and accurately.

    e. Watch it closely and carefully again.

    f. And so on, as long as necessary, until you've finally come up with the best and wisest resolution.

9. The first chance you get, analyze the few poor decisions and solutions you've come up with. See where you went wrong. And the next time you have to make a decision or solve a problem, profit from those mistakes.

MAKE YOURSELF AVAILABLE TO YOUR BOSS

It's true, of course, that you will successfully fulfill your assignments with a minimum of recourse to your superior. But you do have the obligation of being in touch with him for at least the following reasons:

1. To make appropriate suggestions to him for the greater profitability of your efforts.

2. To keep him properly informed of your progress at intervals which *he* finds desirable.

3. To be with him when and where he wants you—promptly and for the length of time required.

I'll now take up each of these obligations.

Make Suggestions Wisely

You most certainly will feel like making suggestions to your boss, from time to time, about:

- Why you shouldn't do what he's asked you to.
- Doing it differently or better.
- Doing something he hasn't asked you to do for which you'd need his approval.
- Some new, different or better way of making your activities—or his or someone else's—more profitable to the company.

Think Before You Suggest

Before you tell him your suggestion you'd do well to stop and ask yourself:

—Is the suggestion important (or potentially important) enough to justify taking up his time?

—Have I thought it through sufficiently to have all possible facets of the idea at my fingertips?

—Have I been making too many suggestions to him lately?

—What is his attitude likely to be toward my making this suggestion to him?

—How can I present it to him in the most favorable light?

Decide Whether to Approach Him

From the answers to these questions you'll be able to judge whether you meet what I consider the *Four Basic Criteria* for making suggestions to your boss:

1. Make only those suggestions which are or can be important enough to justify the effort and the time involved.

2. Be sparing in the number of suggestions you make to him over any period of time. Excessively frequent suggestions may belittle their importance or his evaluation of you.

3. If you do make a suggestion, be armed with all available facts, opinions, documents and/or things pertinent to it.

4. Choose the best time, place and method for presenting your suggestion.

Be Ready for a Rejection

When you make a suggestion to your boss, be prepared to have him turn it down. If he does:

• Accept the rejection graciously.
• Do the very best you can in the light of it.
• Issue orders or instructions to your subordinates, which may grow out of the rejection, as though they were your own—fully and wholeheartedly.
• The next time you have a good suggestion, try again.

KEEP YOUR BOSS PROPERLY INFORMED

A manager must always establish and maintain just the right balance between:

—Keeping out of his boss's way so the latter can get his own work done; and

—Keeping his boss properly and sufficiently informed of his own and his subordinates' progress.

Be Jealous of His Time

Here are *Five Criteria* for judging whether and when to let your immediate superior know the progress you're making:

1. Report to him promptly on all matters regarding which he has asked you to keep him informed by specific deadlines.

A good example of this is the foreman who sends in his daily man-hours report within half an hour after the workmen have gone home.

2. Report to him on succeeding stages of your progress, on a specific job, only if the segments of your communication represent something he really should know at that time.

For instance, suppose you've made a minor change in the sequence of your operations. You're confident that it's within your authority to do so. You know that the modification is sound. But news of the variation could be of importance to Production Control and Materials Handling. So, you play it safe and let your boss know what you've done.

3. If something unusual comes up of an important nature, let him know about it just as soon as you can.

Illustration: You've sent in a requisition for more pallets. Word has come back to you that you won't be able to get them for a week. Your present production schedule will make those pallets essential in two days. While continuing with your plans you tell the boss about this problem.

4. If the job is running on a tight schedule, take the initiative, from time to time, to let him know that you're making satisfactory progress.

This will give the boss greater peace of mind. *And,* it will keep him off your back.

5. When the whole job has been satisfactorily completed, let him know that fact—even if he hasn't asked for the information.

Your boss may be too busy to check up on the job as often as he'd like. And he may assume that you haven't finished yet. This could mean his delaying a new assignment for the completion of which he's under some pressure.

Go See Him or Be Where He Wants You

The final responsibility you have, in making yourself available to your boss, is either:

- To go and see him at once, when and where he wants you, and for as long as he wants you; or
- To be where he wants to come and see you, whenever and wherever this may be, and for as long as he wishes it.

Make It Easy for Him

For either or both of these situations you must:

—Be so well organized that you can be with him—with a clear mind —without interfering with your effective management of your whole responsibility; and

—Make it easy for him to find you when and where he needs you. In this connection, whenever you are about to leave your usual place of activity, be sure to leave specific and accurate word—with someone reliable who'll be where your superior will try to contact you—of your intended and actual whereabouts.

TREAT YOUR BOSS RIGHT

While your immediate superior should establish and maintain good relations with *you,* you must do the same for *him.* Even if he is remiss in any way, in meeting this responsibility of his, you must be a perfect subordinate to him.

Be a Realist

The reasons why you should treat him right are:

- He's your boss no matter how he treats *you.*
- While you may make selected suggestions to him, you would do well not to try to change his basic habits, attitudes or tendencies.
- You'll render him a greater service if you get along well with him no matter how badly he gets along with you.

Be Practical

Here are *Six Key Rules* for treating your boss right:

1. Try to understand him: his likes, his dislikes, his standards, his strengths, his weaknesses.

A good example of success in this connection comes from Ron Thatcher.

After each interview with his boss he spent some time in his office for careful analyses. He made a list of the various reactions he noticed when he was with his superior. And he was able to trace specific patterns which characterized his boss's behavior.

Ron carefully planned his approaches to the man above. His batting average for accurate appraisals of mood was pretty high.

2. Avoid doing or saying anything which might set him off against you, or cause him to lose his temper.

Not so astute in this was George Peters.

George's boss had told him repeatedly that he wanted to be consulted before the budget on any one job was overrun. And George just as often committed himself to all the expenditure necessary in order to get the job done, even though it exceeded budget.

The fact that George's decision generally turned out to be justifiable in no way altered his boss's displeasure. He wanted to be consulted, and George either forgot to do so or didn't think it important at the time.

3. Never, *never, Never* tell him what's wrong with him, even—especially—if he asks you to.

Avoid like the plague the invitation: "I want you to be frank with me. What are my faults?"

He doesn't really want to know, especially from you. Just tell him you hadn't noticed any.

4. If he speaks to you, or behaves toward you, in a manner which is less than pleasant or friendly, try very hard to overlook it.

Just act as though he'd been behaving in a matter-of-fact way. Above all, don't answer or react in kind! Pay strict attention to the *substance* of what he says, and pay *no* attention to *how* he says it.

5. No matter how he treats you, always be courteous, respectful and cordial to him.

If you really can't take it, try to get a different job in the company, without jeopardizing your relationship to him should you not get the transfer.

But if you're going to stay in that department, you might as well get along with *him*, even if *he* doesn't get along with *you*.

6. Don't let any attitude you might have toward him affect the excellence of your work performance.

A good illustration of how a man is judged on his attitudes toward his superiors is the following case.

An executive was interviewing a number of people for a vacant position in his department. Several of the application blanks revealed candidates who were excessive job-hoppers. One of them gave, as his reason for leaving every job, "My boss was impossible to get along with."

The interviewing executive made sure that that applicant would never be able to say the same thing about him.

DO SUCCESSFULLY EVERYTHING HE EXPECTS OF YOU

You still have one more responsibility toward your boss before you can be satisfied that you're working effectively with him.

Take These Steps First

- Find out what he expects of you.
- Find out how to do this successfully.
- Line up your "profit tools."
- Make your own decisions.
- Make yourself available to your boss.
- Treat him right.

Then Do This:

Consistently complete, to his entire satisfaction, everything he asks you to do.

You're not really working effectively with your boss:

—If you succeed in all of the six factors outlined just above, but

—Fail in any respect to do a completely satisfactory job.

Strive for Perfection

The final test in this *Success Factor* is the kind of *results* you achieve by following the best principles and practices.

In pursuit of this goal you should avoid remarks like these, made by some managers:

"I don't know why he's squawking. I did the best I could."

"Sure. I didn't finish on time, but it wasn't my fault."

A Case in Point

An example of the *wrong* attitude toward results is Bill Horan.

He had recently been named Branch Manager. His boss almost daily had to call Bill's attention to one or another oversight that could and should have been avoided.

The new Branch Manager's retort, after a week of this, was:

"I don't see why you're so upset. I don't do the *same* thing wrong twice. Every time I do something wrong, it's a different thing altogether."

Anticipate Obstacles

Suppose you're working on an assigned job. Something comes up which you can't prevent. You're quite sure it will keep you from completing the task to your boss's entire satisfaction. *Point this out to him* the very moment you become aware of or suspect this. And, preferably, be prepared with an explanation of steps you plan to take to minimize its harmful effects.

Seek Necessary Help

Also, suppose you feel you can't do exactly what the boss wants of you without his help or advice. Go right up to him and ask for it.

But, within whatever limitations may be imposed on you, your duty to your boss is unequivocally this:

FINISH THE JOB: —On time.
                       —Strictly according to specs.
                       —Completely within budget.

SUCCESS CAPSULE NUMBER FIVE

In *Success Factor Number Five* you make a valuable contribution to management (and your own advancement) by *Working effectively with your boss.*

How to achieve this important objective? By fulfilling the following responsibilities toward your superior:

1. Meet him more than half-way.
2. Find out exactly what he expects of you. Be tactful in the steps you take in this inquiry.
3. Find out how to do successfully what he expects of you.
4. Line up the facilities you'll need in order to carry out his wishes to his entire satisfaction.
5. As far as possible, make your own decisions, and solve your own problems. If you feel you want to consult your boss first, do so. But be armed with well-thought-out alternative decisions or solutions.
6. Make yourself available to your boss.
7. Make wise suggestions to him—wisely.
8. Keep your boss informed of your progress—at proper intervals.
9. Be where your boss wants you *when* he wants you.
10. Treat your boss right, regardless of whether *he* treats *you* right.
11. Do successfully everything he expects of you. Keep to a bare unavoidable minimum the times when you must explain to him your reason for *not* succeeding. *Report* on *success,* and *back it up* with *success.*

How You Can Get Along with Your Colleagues

This *Success Factor* helps you establish and maintain the most profitable teamwork possible. It seeks to prevent your colleagues from making statements like these:

"I thought *he* was supposed to do that."
"Hey, that's *my* responsibility, not yours."
"He just won't cooperate with me."
"That's *his* affair, not mine."

The attitudes behind such remarks keep many jobs from getting done on time and cause others to cost more than they should. Meanwhile, the balding boss tears out what's left of his hair.

Work on Teamwork

There must be times when you'd give your eye-teeth to get the whole-hearted cooperation of one or more of your colleagues. Of course, "it takes two to tango." A really well-coordinated team increases and improves the personal effectiveness and efficiency of every one on it.

PINPOINT YOUR "LINE AND STAFF" RELATIONSHIPS

You may remember that old baseball gag about *who's* on first and *what's* on second. But it's not funny when a man doesn't know who are the others on his team and what position he plays on it.

85

Know Your Teammates

While the present *Success Factor* concentrates on your *lateral* relationships, let's first examine certain aspects of your overall contacts. This brief self-test will help you sort out and describe some of your upwards, sidewards and downwards relationships.

Question	Answer
1. Who's my immediate superior?	
2. Is he the only one with whom I have that relationship?	
3. With how many people on my own level do I have frequent or periodic relationships?	
4. How often do I fail to get their full cooperation?	
5. How often do I fail to cooperate fully with them?	
6. Do I ever run into a problem with an executive on a higher level than mine (not my immediate superior) who wants me to do something for him?	
7. Do I ever cause such a problem for someone on a lower level than mine who is not a subordinate of mine?	

Your answers to this questionnaire will probably reveal one or more problems which prevent smooth relationships, problems which you face almost daily. The solution to such problems, and many other teamwork difficulties, rests on a sound understanding and pursuit of correct "line and staff" relationships.

Start with a Chart

Study Chart 1. It's the basis of the explanation which follows it.

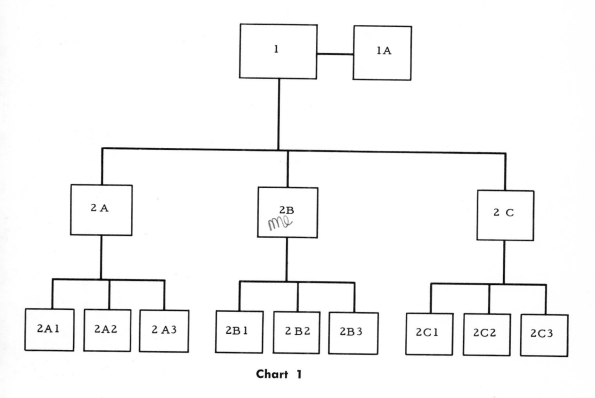

Chart 1

Suppose, for the moment, that this diagram represents a portion of your own company's organizational structure. And assume that *your* position is 2B. Here is where you stand regarding the people around you.

"Toe the Line"

1. You have what is generally called a *line* relationship with all those people whose position boxes are connected with your own—between the *center* of one box and the *center* of the other—by:

a. Either a *straight* line;

b. Or a *right-angle* line in one continuous direction.

For example, you would have a *line* relationship, according to Chart 1, with *only* the following positions:

1, 2B1, 2B2, 2B3

Respect the "Staff"

2. You have what is generally called a *staff* relationship with every-one else on Chart 1.

Thus, you—as 2B—have a *staff* relationship with *all* of these positions (and *only* these):

    a. 1A

    b. 2A

    c. 2A1, 2A2, 2A3 (and *all* of *their* respective *line* subordinates, if any)

    d. 2C

    e. 2C1, 2C2, 2C3 (and *all* of *their* respective *line* subordinates, if any)

FOLLOW THE LINE PROPERLY

Here are the guidelines for the proper pursuit of line relationships:

- A higher position has complete and exclusive authority over its immediate subordinate positions.
- Anything that 2B, for example, asks 2B1, 2B2 and 2B3 to do regarding company affairs, they are required to do.
- 2B is completely and exclusively responsible for 2B1, 2B2 and 2B3 (and, through them, for *all* of their respective line subordinates), and accountable to 1 (and only 1) for this responsibility.
- 2B1, 2B2 and 2B3 are, each one of them, responsible and account-able only to 2B, for everything that is done (or not properly done) by themselves or their respective line subordinates.
- As a general rule, 2B1, 2B2 and 2B3 will communicate, in a line capacity, only with 2B.

MAXIMIZE "STAFF" RELATIONS

It's inevitable that a particular word should popularly come to have more than one meaning, each one proper for the person using it in his own way. The only trouble is that, when this happens, somebody's liable to become confused.

Unfortunately, the word *staff* has suffered this fate.

An Illustration

As I sat listening to a Department Manager one day, I heard him say: "I'm calling a staff meeting for tomorrow, at 9 A.M." The people he had in mind *all* reported to him in a *line* capacity. While he was privileged to use the word *staff* as he did, he was really referring to his immediate *line* subordinates.

Another Example

In one company the Personnel Manager kept on saying that he held a *staff* position. What he meant was that his relationship with the rest of the employees was *predominantly* staff.

Meaning of "Staff"

In the discussion which is to follow I use the word *staff* in its strictest sense, free of the popular variations described above.

Give "Staff" Relations Their Proper Impetus

Here are *Two Keys* to establishing and maintaining the best kinds of staff relationships:

1. Anyone may ask anyone else, with whom he has a *staff* relationship, to do something for or with him. (2A may, for example, try to persuade 2B to "lend" him three men for a particular job.) He may cajole, beg or entreat. The only thing he shouldn't do is "order" the other to do so.

2. The one asked may comply, if he judges that this is proper and feasible, but he *doesn't have to do so*. (If 2A feels that 2B really *should* do as 2A asks, the latter must present his case to 1, who decides what's to be done.)

START THE TEAMWORK ROLLING

Your proper use of staff relationships is the clue to *initiating* teamwork. It's not enough for you to *respond* favorably to requests from others for cooperation. You have a strong responsibility to seek and secure the collaboration of your staff-related colleagues.

Achieve Teamwork Success

You'll get maximum/optimum teamwork results if you:

- Know and understand your own organizational structure thoroughly and accurately.
- Know *who's* supposed to do *what,* as this may affect you, and *when* and *how* he's expected to do it.
- Know whom you have a right to call on for *staff* cooperation.
- Know which people in your own immediate organization should be called on for help before you go higher up to seek it.

MEET YOUR LATERAL OBLIGATIONS

Here are three of the more important ways in which you can *initiate* desirable staff-related teamwork:

1. Optimize Interpersonal Relations

Make it your business to get along well with your colleagues, no matter how difficult this may be.

And, as you know, some people *are* difficult to get along with.

An Anecdote

You may remember the story of the young wife who made her husband promise to wear one of the two ties her mother had given him for Christmas, since she was coming to dinner that night. When that fine old lady arrived, she kissed her daughter and son-in-law and then asked him:

"What's the matter? Didn't you like the other tie I gave you?"

Take the Initiative

You might say: "Why should *I* have to get along well with a person who is so difficult to get along with?"

The answer is that you've got to work with him anyway. And you'll get much better cooperation from him if the interpersonal relationship between the two of you is smooth.

Besides, you'll enjoy the collaboration much more if the air between you is pleasant. This, in turn, is bound to increase your own effectiveness, as well as his.

Get the Ball Rolling

Here are *Four Keys* to establishing and maintaining, with a colleague, the kind of interrelationships I'm recommending:

- Always be cordial to him, regardless of how he reacts to you.
- Approach him tactfully, with humility, respectfully and with dignity.
- Ask him whether he'd "be good enough" to do what you want him to do, and express your gratitude adequately.
- If he shows you any animus, hostility or displeasure, don't react to it; *stick to* the matters at hand.

The Fruits of Poor Relationships

Here is a case I came across which illustrates the unhappy results of *not* practicing these principles.

Ralph Walters was Superintendent of Supply for an airline overhaul base. Oscar Mayer was Superintendent of Fusilage Assembly.

Oscar's foremen complained that Ralph's Parts Clerks made them wait too long before they filled requisitions. Ralph's clerks complained that Oscar's foremen didn't use the official parts numbers, relying, rather, on seat-of-the-pants descriptions of what they wanted.

Ralph said he wouldn't order his men to fill the requisitions until Oscar's foremen used the right numbers. Oscar said his foremen didn't have the time to bother to look the numbers up, that the Parts Clerks were acting the way they did just because Oscar and Ralph didn't get along personally.

The unnecessary cost to the company—in waiting, and in resulting overtime—was considerable.

2. Give as Well as Take

Cooperate fully with those from whom you expect, want or need cooperation.

Here are some steps which can be taken to assure such cooperation:

—Do whatever you reasonably can in response to a request for cooperation from a colleague.

—If you think that he may need your help, but hasn't asked you for it, tactfully suggest your services (if this is consistent with your other responsibilities).

—If you *must* turn down someone's request for cooperation, do so (with reasons) in the most tactful and gracious way possible, urging him to call on you again, and promising that you'll try to work with him the next time.

3. Pinpoint Your Initiative-Responsibility

Somebody has to have the responsibility for *initiating* an activity requiring the cooperation of two or more people. Make it *your* responsibility always to find out or know exactly what joint actions must be started by *you*.

Here are some of the questions you should ask yourself in order to make sure of meeting this responsibility.

a. What am I supposed to do or say to—or regarding—others, without any prodding or reminder from them?

b. What am I supposed to say, give or send to others on my own steam?

c. To whom? When? How?

An Unfortunate Case

Here's an example of the unsatisfactory fulfillment of initiative-responsibility, one that I came across in one of my client companies.

Warren Henry was Maintenance Superintendent for a national van-line company. The official procedure required him to notify the dispatcher, Norm Owens, just as soon as a van was ready to leave the preventive maintenance garage for the loading pool.

At least twice a week Norm needed every vehicle the company owned. When the pool was completely empty, Norm consulted his record of vehicles in preventive maintenance. Not a week went by that Norm didn't have this kind of conversation with Warren:

"Hey, Warren, shouldn't Vehicle X be ready for me by now?"

"Yeah, sure, Norm. We finished it hours ago. Want to send for it?"

FOLLOW THROUGH ON LATERAL REQUESTS

You can help assure the kind of teamwork you're seeking if you'll follow up on all requests you make of your colleagues. You'll have to be tactful, of course, in reminding any staff-related person of something he promised to do for you by a certain time. But at least you ought to know when the cooperation is due so you'll be able to go after anything not sent you in keeping with deadlines.

Record All Important Promises

Here's a mechanical device which can help you remember *who* promised *what* and *when*.

Draw up a chart something like the accompanying one.

Date I must have the work in my hands	Date promised for sending it to me	Nature of the work	Undertaken by	On

Check Daily

At the beginning of each business day look at the first column of your chart, and go after any work not sent to you by a promised date. This date should generally precede your own obligation sufficiently so that if you don't get the work early enough you can still do it yourself (or make other arrangements) before your own deadline.

FOLLOW THROUGH ON LATERAL PROMISES

You can, additionally, help promote desirable teamwork by meeting your own staff-related promises promptly and properly.

Take Prompt Remedial Action

If there is a chance that you won't be able to do so, you should take this kind of action:

1. Just as soon as it begins to look as though you may not be able to keep your promise, or meet the promised deadline, notify your colleague of that fact.

2. Apologize to him and tell him why it happened.

3. Assure him that you'll get it to him just as soon as possible, and offer to do anything reasonable to make up for the failure to stick to the original schedule.

Take Prompt Delivery Action

Just as soon as you know when you'll be ready to give someone what you owe him, plan for its prompt and efficient delivery.

- Either notify him that it's ready (or that it will be by a specified date and time) in a specified place—if that's what's called for;
- Or (if you don't already know) find out when, where and how he wants it delivered, and see to it that it gets there precisely that way.

Don't make the mountain come to Mohammed.

MAKE ONLY IMPORTANT SUGGESTIONS

Avoid that diminution in the effectiveness of your lateral relationships which can come from over-zealousness in company responsibility. Consider this situation, which you doubtless encounter from time to time:

You see one of your colleagues or, worse still, one of his subordinates doing something wrong. It really doesn't affect your own functioning or effectiveness. You're very conscientious and loyal to your company. You really want to be helpful. So you go ahead and point out to him where he erred and how he can do it better.

In such a situation I'd like to offer a word of advice: *"Don't!"* Limit your suggestions to situations justifying them.

For Example

In one of my client companies, Frank Marsh was always telling people over whom he had no line authority how they could do better, whatever it was he noticed them doing. Only a few of Frank's observations dealt with activities of any importance at all. Most of them were trivial. Besides, they were really none of Frank's business.

But Frank had a "suggestion-compulsion." He just *had to* point out to others their departures from perfection.

Result? Frank grew very unpopular and got precious little cooperation from others. Moreover, in the few cases where it really *was* important for Frank to point out areas of improvement for others, they were pre-conditioned to paying him no attention.

Make Suggestions Judiciously

Fortunately, there *is* a way of being helpful to those who need your advice, without antagonizing them.

Try this experiment for a month:

• Before you call a colleague's attention to an error, an imperfection or an oversight, ask yourself whether it really concerns you. If it doesn't, ask yourself whether he's liable to resent your pointing it out to him. Decide just how important it is to the company for *you* to apprise him of a way in which he can improve his performance. Then, unless there are some compelling reasons to the contrary, don't say anything about it.

• If you notice something in a colleague that calls for improvement, and you judge that it *is* advisable to talk to him about it, approach the matter somewhat like this:

Make Suggestions Properly

1. Ask his pardon for introducing the subject.
2. Assure him that you're doing so only in the interest of being of assistance to him.
3. Convince him that you feel and intend no criticism of him personally.
4. Ask him whether your analysis of the matter at hand is accurate.
5. Tactfully make your suggestion.

Back Down Where Advisable

If he shows any resentment at your remarks, try to get back into his good graces and don't pursue the matter any further. If it still requires attention, try other channels, depending on how serious it is.

   a. If it's important enough, invite him to join you (through channels) before a common boss, to discuss the matter.

   b. If he doesn't go for that, and it's really a serious matter, tell him you're sorry that you'll have to go to your boss about it.

WELCOME YOUR COLLEAGUES' SUGGESTIONS

You will receive two kinds of suggestions from colleagues: one kind, valid; the other, not valid. I'd like to talk about the second kind first, starting with a pertinent experience I once had.

Always Listen Attentively

When I was Director of the Consulting and Training Division of a multi-service company, I had about a dozen consultants and trainers reporting to me. Among them was Bert.

Bert was a real nice guy. We all liked him. And he was quite a competent trainer. There was only one major flaw in Bert's make-up: he was very vain. He liked to shine and to be seen shining.

The first time Bert attended a meeting of all the consultants and trainers who worked for me, he made a suggestion which was really impractical. I pointed this out. Bert clung to his idea stubbornly, and I couldn't change his opinion. He still thought his plan very feasible. A lot of valuable meeting time was taken up by this useless interchange.

I learned my lesson.

Thereafter, this was what regularly happened with Bert at our periodic 2-hour meetings:

First Hour: Bert sat with a very thoughtful look on his face. No wonder! He was thinking up his regular suggestion.

Early Part of Second Hour: Bert made a suggestion whose only purpose was, quite obviously, to show how deep a thinker he was. It had no merit in my eyes.

Immediately Thereafter: I paused for a moment, seemed to consider the idea, and said something like: "That's a very interesting thought, Bert. Let me note it down and get back to you on it." (I never did and never had to.)

Rest of the Meeting: Not a peep out of Bert. He was very happy. He'd had his unchallenged moment in the sun.

Handle Suggestions Wisely

Avoid these *Five Hazards to Rapport* with your suggesting colleagues:
1. Failure to listen when a colleague makes a suggestion.
2. An outward manifestation of an unfavorable reaction to his suggestion.
3. Arguing with him that his suggestion is not a good one.
4. Failure to thank him for it or make him feel that you consider it at least worth thinking about.
5. Failure to follow a good suggestion when it's made.

Follow Up on Good Suggestions

When one of your colleagues makes a suggestion to you that you consider valid:
—Thank him for it.
—Act on it in keeping with your own standards of performance and responsibility.
—Let him know of the *good* things that came from his suggestion.

FILL YOUR TEAM POSITION PROPERLY

Your final responsibility toward your colleagues—and your company—is to:
- Take proper care of all of *your* position responsibilities, without:
- Unauthorizedly duplicating the work of someone else on the team.

SUCCESS CAPSULE NUMBER SIX

This *Success Factor* gave you some guidance on how to establish and maintain the proper teamwork with your colleagues. It emphasized the following points:
1. Know your "Line and Staff" relationships thoroughly and accurately.
2. Follow the line properly and deal appropriately with your "staff-related" colleagues.
3. Take the proper initiative in instituting and following through on teamwork.

4. Make sure to get along well with all your colleagues, no matter what efforts they make toward you in this respect.

5. Follow through—tactfully—on the fulfillment of cooperation promised you by staff-related colleagues.

6. Meet your own lateral promises: promptly, correctly and completely.

7. Limit your suggestions to staff-related colleagues, to those which are really worthwhile, and make them tactfully.

8. Be receptive to the suggestions of your colleagues, even if you're not going to use them.

How You Can Successfully Man Your Department

This *Success Factor* treats your responsibility for always having a full complement of competent, effective people reporting to you. It emphasizes how you can profitably achieve this objective.

You must have heard, in your own experience, remarks like these:

"I don't have enough mechanics to keep up with all the work thrown on me."

"Yesterday he was an operator and today he's a foreman. I didn't even have time to train him."

"I had to hire a Laboratory Supervisor from the outside. I just didn't have anyone I could promote."

Were the complainers justified? Could they have avoided their difficulties?

This is what I will now take up.

MAKE A "HELP WANTED" INVENTORY

You will want to avoid the mistake made by many management men, who fail to start early enough in their plans for filling positions or jobs in

99

Position (job) title

SPECIFICATIONS

Age: between _____ and _____

Minimum formal education:

Minimum previous experience:

Minimum knowledge:

Minimum skills:

Other requirements:

MINIMUM STANDARDS OF PERFORMANCE

Task	Standards

their departments. You can begin to tackle your manning problem by asking yourself these questions:

- What jobs or positions in my department are now, or soon will be, unfilled or poorly filled?
- How much productivity can I expect from anyone who fills the jobs or positions in my department?
- What kinds of people do I want for these jobs (positions) and where do I get them?

Plan Your Manpower Needs

Here's a suggested approach to meeting your manpower needs:

1. Pre-print cards with the kind of format and contents shown in the sample given on page 100.

2. Fill out a card for each kind of position or job in your department, present or contemplated.

To help you fill in the *Minimum Standards of Performance* section of the card, here is a suggested procedure:

- a. Break each job down into its basic units of work required; for example: rivets to be hammered, letters to be typed, customers to be waited on, experiments to be coordinated, etc.
- b. Observe how long it takes one or more reliable and productive employees to finish a given number of units satisfactorily. If necessary, do some of the work yourself and assume that you work a little faster than your more reliable men.
- c. Strike an average of the number of units you think a reasonably competent and conscientious employee can satisfactorily complete in an hour, day, week, etc., according to whatever period of time is most meaningful to you.

3. Whenever you're ready to plan the *numbers* of people you may need, use a form like that on page 102.

4. To help you decide the *number* of people you will need for any one position or job for any particular period of time:

- a. Estimate the total number of units of work you'll need for that job (position) for that period of time;
- b. Divide the total number of units by the average number of units one man can satisfactorily complete.

5. Before you decide to look outside your department or company for any new or additional men, see whether you have any men now working for you who would qualify.

I offer here, a suggested method for continually evaluating your

Date when needed	Job (position) title	Number of people needed	Remarks

present subordinates for this purpose. (It can, incidentally, also be used for other evaluation goals.)

The system involves, simply, pre-printing forms like that given on page 104, filling out a form for each of your present subordinates, and keeping it up to date.

6. If you decide to seek candidates outside of your department (or company), the procedure is, again, quite simple:

    a. For the position or job in question, refer to the card mentioned in 1.

    b. Determine the number of people you need for each such job (position), as in 3. and 4.

    c. Recruit candidates through established channels and use the criteria, referred to in 1., as a guide to your selection.

RECRUIT EARLY AND OFTEN

You want to make sure you'll be able to get all the men you need *when* you need them. Here are, first, some examples of how others have successfully achieved this result:

An Engineering Illustration

Take the case of a Project Engineer whom I know.

He has been using four Responsibility Engineers during the last year. He hasn't been given any indication that his manpower needs for the next few months will increase. But he's been through many situations where he suddenly found himself shorthanded.

He's therefore constantly in touch with other Project Engineers in his company. He knows approximately how many Responsibility Engineers they may be able to release to him in case of an emergency.

What's more, he's met all of those men personally. When he needs more Responsibility Engineers he'll have little trouble locating good people right away.

A Retailing Illustration

Dan Palmer is the Merchandise Manager for his classification of department store goods.

Assistant Buyers frequently get discouraged or become impatient about their opportunities to become buyers. The turnover of Assistant Buyers is fairly high.

Dan has a standing order in with the Store's Personnel Director that

| Employee's Name | | | | | Number | | |

| Position (Job) Title |

| Record of Compliance with Performance Requirements |

Requirements	Dates of evaluations	Satisfactory (S) or Unsatisfactory (U)	If *U*, does he warrant an additional period of trial? (*Yes* or *No*.) (If *Yes*, fill in next columns.)	Dates of next evaluations	S or U	Additional trial?	Etc.
Job knowledge							
Job skills							
Attitudes							
Compliance with performance standards							
Compliance with policies and procedures							
Other (specify)							

he's in the market for bright young people from other ends of the business who might qualify for Assistant Buyers' jobs.

And Dan doesn't wait until vacancies occur. He interviews all likely prospects and maintains a file on them.

Fix Five Focuses

You'll be ahead of the manpower game if you follow these suggestions:

1. Always have a fairly good idea of how many people you or your immediate subordinates are going to need in the near future.

2. Either by yourself or, if the needs are your immediate subordinate's, through the latter, maintain a continuing program of seeking qualified candidates for the positions or jobs in question. Do this by:

    a. Constantly reviewing the people you now have, to see who might qualify for the jobs or positions in question; *and*

    b. Get to know the people in departments other than your own who might qualify; *and*

    c. Let your company's Personnel Director know what your needs are and are likely to be, urging him to keep on referring to you people who might qualify.

3. Without making any promises to anyone, interview all candidates and find out:

    a. Whether they really qualify for the positions or jobs in question.

    b. Whether they'd be interested in being kept on your waiting list, without obligation either way, until a suitable vacancy occurs.

    c. Whether they're free to make a change without offending either your colleagues or another company with which you want to maintain good relations.

4. Notify those who favorably meet all of the above conditions that you'll let them know just as soon as a vacancy occurs.

5. When it does occur, go to that list and take the best candidates still available and interested.

RECRUIT IN DEPTH

You are responsible for proper recruitment all the way down in your department. Thus, if you have subordinates who must themselves recruit, you'll have to make sure that they know how to do this well, and actually *do* it well.

Here are two cases which show, respectively, the results of poor and/or effective in-depth manpower planning.

An Example of Unsatisfactory Coverage

The month was July. The plant had begun its vacation schedule. Production was tapering off.

Dick Redmond was looking forward to a three-week auto trip with his family. He was slated to leave on August 5th. And leave he did.

In his instructions to the superintendent who was to take his place while he was gone, Dick said nothing about manpower needs for September.

Dick got back the day after Labor Day to find that Production Control had assigned a heavier workload to his department than for the previous fall seasons.

Dick just didn't have on tap the manpower he needed to meet the new demands being made on him. And it wasn't easy at that time of year to get the kind of help he required.

An Example of Satisfactory Coverage

This next case was told me by the manager of a store in a supermarket chain.

"One year, in April, I learned that a large manufacturer of transformers expected to open up his new plant in my community early in July. I had made it my business to find out that they would employ many young people for routine assembly jobs, requiring no previous experience.

"I also had good reason to believe that they'd pay a little more for their people than we did for our clerks and other service people. I anticipated a concentrated drive on the part of the new company's Personnel Department to woo people away from other businesses in the neighborhood.

"I called a meeting of my Department Managers, described the situation to them, and alerted them to their probable manpower needs for July.

"As a result of this meeting we got some very good ideas on how to cope with the problem. Each one of my Department Managers started a recruitment drive right away.

"While we didn't hire any new people at once, we had them all lined up as prospective candidates. A number of them were high school seniors at the time.

"When the drain on our manpower began, we had enough people to call on so that we could continue to do business as usual. We even had time to break in the new clerks so that they weren't entirely green in their new jobs."

CONTROL YOUR SPAN

You must effectively guide and supervise *all* of your immediate subordinates. And each one of *them* must do the same for *his* immediate subordinates. This goes on, of course, all the way down your line.

And it's *your* responsibility to see to it that this responsibility is properly met all the way down that line.

This brings up the question: How many subordinates can any one manager effectively manage?

Don't Look for a Fixed Number

In my experience I've never found anyone who could definitely state a specific, maximum number of people that any one management man can effectively control, regardless of his company or position. As you would expect, this number varies from type of activity to type of activity.

Plan Your Own Span

The only criteria I can suggest for deciding *your* best span of control are:
- Stick to the ideal of maximum delegation.
- Have enough immediate subordinates so that they can, among them, meet all of the responsibilities you've delegated.
- Limit that number so that you can devote all the time necessary for properly managing each one and all of them, in addition to your other, non-delegable activities.
- If the above recommendations mean that you may need *too many* immediate subordinates, give some thought to whether your department has too many things to do. If so, maybe you can arrange to be relieved of the excess responsibilities.

Plan the Span in Depth

You'll also want to make sure that your subordinate management people, all the way down the line, have suitable Spans of Control. You can accomplish this by making it clear to your *immediate* subordinates that each one of them has the same *span* responsibility for *his* subordinates as you do for all of yours.

Point out to them, also, that they'll have to see to it that this message is effectively passed on all the way down the management line of your department.

SUCCESS CAPSULE NUMBER SEVEN

This *Success Factor* dealt with your downward *manning* responsibilities, and suggested the following action to be taken by you:

1. Make an inventory of the people your department needs or may need.
2. Recruit to fill these needs: early and often.
3. Anticipate your future manpower needs and line up potential, desirable candidates.
4. Make sure that every one of your immediate management subordinates effectively plans and fulfills his *own* manpower needs.
5. Plan the most effective and efficient Span of Control possible for your department. And see to this not only for your immediate subordinates, but also, through them, for your whole subordinate line.

How You Can Delegate without Losing Control

This *Success Factor* takes up your responsibility for delegating as much as possible, and shows how this can be done effectively. To introduce the subject, here's an example of the problem this *Success Factor* will help you avoid.

Don't Do It All Yourself

It happened at an Oil Refinery.

Alfred Courtney was Chief Chemist. As I observed him for a few weeks, I couldn't help noticing how busy he always was.

He'd be testing samples, writing reports, conducting experiments . . . in short, he was having a good time. These were the activities closest to his heart.

"Bill," he told me one day, "I can't seem to get the kind of chemists I need for my department. Look at the work they turn out. See how impure these samples are."

In the entire two-week period that I spent with him, I never once saw him go out of his office and into the refinery to talk with his subordinates. Nor did he walk about among the chemists themselves.

But busy? To look at him, you'd think he was one of his company's greatest assets.

Don't Join the Club

There are many similar examples of conscientious, well-intentioned executives who are members of the "Do-It-Yourself" Club. And they don't even realize that they're spending the bulk of their time improperly, and unprofitably for the company.

Evaluate Yourself

Try this True-False Test, with yourself as the subject. Then, when you've finished reading this *Success Factor,* come back and check your answers to see whether you are delegating properly.

Statement	*T*	*F*
1. I spend most of my time in my office.		
2. I do some of the same kind of work as my immediate subordinates.		
3. I can rely on my immediate subordinates to get their work done without my supervision.		
4. The only work I do by myself is what I can't delegate to anyone else.		
5. My boss is satisfied with the way in which I get my work done.		

DELEGATE AS MUCH AS POSSIBLE

You must, of course, do a great deal of work yourself. As a matter of fact, you'll really be earning your salary if you're so busy that you can't find the time to count the money you earn. But you'll be *earning* it if you fill your business day with only those activities which are consistent with the level and importance of your position.

Three Golden Rules

Here are some important guidelines for doing your job well.

RULE NUMBER ONE: Plan your responsibilities in such a way that you can effectively delegate to your immediate subordinates the day-to-day implementation of *practically all* of the work involved in your department.

An Illustration

In one company which I served as a consultant I saw the two opposite viewpoints on delegation represented by two executives.

One of them didn't subscribe to the principle of almost total delegation. He maintained that it was his job to "work right along with" his people. When I asked him how much time he had for creative thinking, planning and evaluation, he replied that he had very little.

The other told me that he almost never did anything which one of his subordinates was employed to do. He claimed that he spent at least 25% of his day thinking about his department, planning for improvements and growth, and evaluating progress.

RULE NUMBER TWO: Then *delegate* to your immediate subordinates *practically all* of your own responsibility. But remember that in doing so you don't lose *any* of your *own* responsibility. This is a fact of business life which defies the normal laws of mathematics.

Here's how it works:

1. Break the sum total of your responsibilities down into groups, so that each group fits the position description of one of your immediate subordinates.

2. Assign to each of those subordinates that group of responsibilities most appropriate to him, trying to leave yourself with nothing to do regarding those responsibilities.

3. Supervise your subordinates fulfillment of those responsibilities to make sure that they meet them to your entire satisfaction.

4. Be prepared to do by yourself those few things which they may not be able to accomplish exactly as you want them.

5. Always hold yourself *exclusively* and *completely* responsible and accountable to your own boss for every one of your own responsibilities which you have delegated to your immediate subordinates.

RULE NUMBER THREE: Make sure to delegate to your immediate subordinates *absolutely all* of the *authority* they'll need in order to carry out their responsibilities effectively. And I recommend that you spell this out to them very clearly. They must not only *have* the authority, they must *know* they have it, and they must *exercise* it: consistently and successfully.

Don't Sidestep Your Authority

You don't lose any of your own authority by delegating pieces of it to your subordinates. You can always overrule them, although you will want to do so only when this is really necessary.

Avoid These Pitfalls

Here are some samples of the kinds of statements made to me by hundreds of management men:

"My boss holds me responsible for everything he assigns to me, but he doesn't give me the authority to get the work done."

"I have to go to him with every decision before I can put it into effect."

"I can't get rid of an incompetent subordinate, but my boss still gives me work for that man to do."

"Even if I make a decision myself, my boss often fails to back me up."

Delegate Authority Properly

Now I know that a number of the above complaints are not entirely justified. But look at it this way:

• If you haven't given a subordinate full authority commensurate with the responsibility you've delegated to him, you really can't expect him to meet that responsibility satisfactorily.

• If you don't want to give him the necessary authority because you think he isn't capable of assuming or properly exercising it, train him to do so. Or put him into a different kind of job.

• If he's unwilling to exercise the full authority you've delegated to him, make it plain to him that he *must* exercise it or he doesn't belong in that job.

Keep Control of What You Delegate

By all means delegate. But make sure that what you delegate is properly and promptly taken care of.

Here are two relevant situations.

Situation Number One

When I was serving as a consultant to a business equipment manufacturer, I found a major weakness which had been costing them thousands of dollars monthly in lost customers.

The Shipping Department Superintendent quite properly delegated to his subordinates the many important tasks involved in the complicated process of getting the orders out. But he waited until the paperwork reached him before he discovered whether the delivery schedules had been met.

And often this was after a customer had complained that he hadn't received his equipment on the date promised.

Situation Number Two

The following was told to me by an automobile leasing company Department Manager:

> "I have five men reporting to me, each in charge of approximately four supervisors. If I didn't delegate the vast majority of my own responsibilities to them the work would never get done. But it isn't easy. Even though they're all good men, and quite conscientious, they sometimes get bogged down and fall behind in their work. I've got to watch them all the time.
>
> "But still, I'm much better off than if I had to do it all by myself."

Plan Your Controls

Here are *Six Steps* to take in assuring control over what you delegate:

1. *Keep a running record of all work delegated by you to your immediate subordinates.* The chart on page 114 may help you do this effectively.

2. *Every time you delegate a specific task to one of your immediate subordinates, fill in the appropriate spaces on the chart.* Note that for tasks which have to be accomplished in parts there are spaces for each part. You can make your chart as wide as necessary, so that you have enough room for all the information needed for all the segments involved.

Examples

   a. If you ask your General Foreman to have 1500 units of a particular order completed by March 12th, consider 500 units as one segment.

   b. Suppose you've told your Laboratory Head to conduct a pilot experiment with a new process, which you want completed by November 21st. If the experiment can be broken down into four steps, each one requiring successful achievement before you can really begin the next, put down four segments on your chart.

3. *Every business day, as early as possible in the morning, check your chart.* See what deadlines are coming up that day for particular segments of the job.

4. *For every segment-deadline coming up that day, ask yourself whether you're completely satisfied that it is being or has been properly met.* If you're not sure, find out.

Person to whom responsibility was assigned	Nature of the responsibility	Date delegated	Due dates by segment of job					
			Segment	Should be finished by	Checked on	Segment	Should be finished by	Checked on

5. *Where a segment-deadline has not been completely and satisfactorily met:*

    a. Find out why.

    b. Take all necessary steps to make sure that the delay will be made up for, so that the job can proceed according to schedule.

6. *Before the deadline date for the completion of the whole task, check to see whether it's reasonable to assume that it will be completed satisfactorily and on time.* If not, do everything possible to assure such completion. This may require you to:

- Assign additional people to the job.
- Set up different priorities.
- Pitch in yourself.

This is one of the few circumstances where I believe you can feel justified in doing yourself work which more properly belongs to others. But if you have to function that way on a fairly recurring basis, the chances are you don't have the right number and kinds of subordinates.

USE YOUR OWN TIME MOST PROFITABLY

Let me re-state as follows what I've been recommending above:

1. You will, of course, always want to have the proper number and kinds of immediate subordinates called for by your own responsibilities.

2. I think you're better off if you never do by yourself something which can effectively be done by one or more of those subordinates.

Your Possible Questions

It's at this point that you might ask: "Well, if I do that, how am I going to spend my own time? What am *I* going to do all day?"

The Answers

If you delegate to the extent I recommend, you still have more work to do than the number of hours in any business day permits.

I suggest you test that statement against the following compilation of the kinds of responsibilities which you, as a management man have and cannot/should not delegate to others. And if you satisfactorily fulfill *all* of these responsibilities, you'll have no time to do work of a kind which you should delegate to your subordinates.

As you go over the checklist, note your own situation, using the columns left blank for that purpose.

Tasks which I, as a management man must undertake and complete by myself	Number of hours I spend on this in any one day	Number of additional hours this would take me if I had the time to do it properly
1. Being available to my immediate superior whenever the latter wants me.		
2. Maintaining high-level contacts related to my responsibilities with people outside the company.		
3. Communications with people with whom I have staff relations.		
4. Planning the responsibilities I'm going to delegate to my subordinates.		
5. Communicating the delegated tasks to my subordinates.		
6. Motivating my subordinates to do their work with complete satisfaction.		
7. Supervising my subordinates.		
8. Keeping morale high among my subordinates.		
9. Evaluating my subordinates.		
10. Guiding my subordinates in their work and correcting any errors they may commit.		
11. Seeing to it that my subordinates meet all their responsibilities properly and on time.		
12. Making myself available to my subordinates when they wish to consult me.		
13. Planning and carrying out a continuing program of management development and recruitment.		
14. Visiting all employees in my line in order to find out how things are going (and reporting on this to my immediate subordinates) and in order to help boost morale among them.		
15. Reading and analyzing reports from my immediate subordinates and coming to conclusions or decisions regarding them.		
16. Conducting individual interviews and group meetings with my immediate subordinates.		
17. Compiling or drawing up reports to my immediate superior.		
18. Responding to requests by my immediate superior for individual consultation or attendance at meetings.		

Total

SUCCESS CAPSULE NUMBER EIGHT

This *Success Factor* took up your role in the delegation of responsibility and authority, as follows:

1. To delegate to your immediate subordinates everything that they can possibly do or should be able to do.
2. To realize that when you delegate one of your own responsibilities to a subordinate, you still retain 100% of the responsibility delegated.
3. To be sure always to delegate as much *authority* as you do *responsibility*.
4. To keep a record of everything you delegate and check up periodically to see whether the work is progressing satisfactorily.
5. To avoid waiting until the last moment of a deadline by checking up sufficiently in advance so that you can make other arrangements if it begins to look like you may fall behind schedule.

The Third Success Challenge

Maximize Your Productivity

How You Can Control Your Productivity

This *Success Factor* deals with your control of the elements in your department that go to make up profitable productivity. To begin your analysis of how to accomplish this goal, ask yourself these questions:

"Of all the levels of management and non-management in my company, which group can *most* make or break our profit?"

The levels I'm talking about are, roughly, these:

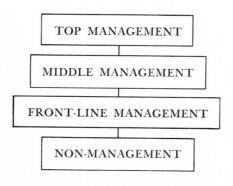

What was your answer?
Mine is: "Non-Management."

121

PINPOINT NON-MANAGEMENT'S PROFIT ROLE

You quite correctly emphasize the importance of Top, Middle and Front-Line Management in profitable productivity. Without those levels of employees there'd be no company and no profits.

But examine the word *management* more closely. What does it really mean?

Management is the action taken by one or more people to *direct* and/or *control* other people (and/or money and things).

Be Only a Manager

As you know, you as a management man have too much to do as a Manager without taking on work which properly belongs to your subordinates. This means that you should be *completely* occupied with *managerial* duties alone.

Delegate Non-Management Work

You need many people to do the actual work which is the backbone of your business. These are your Non-Management people. They are the real "key" to company profit because:

- They actually perform the vast bulk of the work to be done.
- How they do it determines the volume and nature of the company's production (or other results).
- They can cost you too much if you don't watch your step very carefully.
- They may not have the same motivation that you have for doing the right thing all the time.

CAPITALIZE ON THE INPUT-OUTPUT RATIO

Remember the old gag about the commuter who was riding the train to the city one day?

He was tearing bits of newspaper and strewing them out the window as the wheels moved along the track. The conductor, seeing this, started the following conversation with the suburbanite:

> "Excuse me, sir, but why are you throwing pieces of newspaper out the window?"
> "To keep the tigers away from the tracks."
> "There are no tigers on the tracks!"
> "See, it works!"

Silly, isn't it? Yet I've observed many instances, in my visits to companies of all kinds, where Non-Management people are engaged in activities no more useful than what occupied the commuter.

Check Up Frequently

In one of my client companies I saw a laborer busily engaged in shoveling sand from one pile to another. When I asked him what he was doing, and why, he simply described what I had already observed, and said that his foreman had told him to do this.

When I checked with the foreman, I discovered that he had asked him to shovel the sand from a *different* pile, because a need had arisen for only that one pile. The foreman went on to say that he'd been too busy to notice that the laborer was doing the same job on another pile which didn't call for that effort.

Analyze Your Subordinates' Activities

Or take this case.

I was helping a group of management men write a procedure to govern their responsibilities as a group. At one point it came to my attention that for every document typed by the girls in the pool there were two copies more than were needed by that group. The executives to whom the girls had been sending those extra copies had no need for them at all.

See What's Going On

Here's an experience I had in a plant which manufactured condiments.

The Industrial Relations Director was proudly taking me through the section where they made mustard. He pointed out that the process was almost entirely automated. As a matter of fact, I marvelled that there was only one person present in an area where machinery was automatically turning out large quantities of mustard.

What about the one human in the place? She was about fifty years of age, and was stationed at one corner of the complex of modern machinery. At her feet was a large, open sack of mustard seed, containing a hand scoop.

Every few minutes this lady bent down, scooped up a quantity of mustard seed, mounted the top of a case, and poured the seed into the hopper.

SEE YOURSELF AS A COMPANY COST

As you know, you and your entire subordinate line are constantly spending a great deal of your company's money. Some of these costs are fairly fixed, and there's little you or your people can do about lowering them. Other costs, however, can, to a considerable degree, be controlled by the people responsible for incurring them.

Break Down Your Costs

Here's a partial indication of what you and your people may be costing your company. Check this for its applicability to your own situation.

    1. *Fixed or fairly fixed costs.*
- Salaries.
- Full-day, full-week hourly wages.
- Allocated share of company-wide overhead.
- Depreciation of machinery, equipment and tools in your department.

    2. *Variable costs.*
- Repair of premises, machinery, equipment and tools.
- Utilities.
- Materials.
- Materials handling.
- Supplies.
- Overtime pay.

Accept Your Cost Responsibility

You are responsible for seeing to it that you and all your subordinates spend only that amount of company money which is essential for meeting approved productivity goals. Do your subordinates realize and agree that every penny unnecessarily spent by them or *their* subordinates is a waste of company resources?

Pass the Message Along

It's your job to make sure that there are very few company pennies unnecessarily spent, and each of your subordinate levels must effectively pass the message on until it successfully affects your Non-Management people.

This is the essence of your cost-control responsibility.

Get the Work Out—Satisfactorily

Here are two cases which illustrate the importance of fulfilling your *productivity* responsibility.

An Example of Quality-Negligence

In a brush factory where I did some consulting work the Production Superintendent's manufacturing productivity had been lower than forecast. I discovered a number of reasons for this, and was able to help him increase his profitable output. I describe below one illustration of the lower-productivity situation he'd been in.

The wooden blocks for the brushes came into the plant by way of Receiving. There was supposed to be 100% inspection at this point, but sampling was often less expensive, in the long run, than total check.

In one of the manufacturing operations a man was seated at a machine which trimmed the rough edges from the bristles. This man picked up a block (with bristles) from a box to the right of him, put it into the trimming machine and laid it down in a box to his left. I observed him frequently and for extended periods of time.

Never once did I see him looking to discover whether any of the blocks had imperfections.

Hundreds of brushes were returned by customers each day for imperfections in the blocks. Those defects had been there when the blocks were received, remained there through all operations, and were shipped with those same defects. Yet *nobody* caught the unsatisfactory blocks anywhere along the assembly line!

An Example of Quantity-Negligence

This case was brought up while I was conducting a seminar for management men from several different companies.

The Superintendent of the Motor Pool would receive requests from various foremen for vehicles of all kinds, including trucks, to carry materials and/or finished products between the factory and one or another of the warehouses, situated at varying distances from them. When it was discovered that intra-company transportation costs were excessive, as compared to total loads carried, an investigation was made. This revealed that the superintendent was being careless about full-load routing.

A truck could deliver finished products from the factory to a particular warehouse and go back empty to the Pool. An hour later that same truck could be sent to that same warehouse to take raw materials to the factory.

Produce Profitably

You are allocated company money only so you can assure that production of things or creation of services which will ultimately result in profitable sales. Therefore, you must not only see to it that you and your people spend no more of that money than is absolutely necessary; you must make sure that you spend that money to produce or create the most and the best items possible, along lines called for by instructions to you from above.

The key to such results is *profitable human productivity*. This can stem either from the efforts of people alone or from the impact of people on company money and *things* (like machinery, equipment, tools, etc.).

MIND YOUR Q'S, T'S AND C'S

You know that *human productivity* results from the efforts of people. But if those efforts are to be profitable to the company, the efforts *and* the *results* must meet certain *standards*. You can meet your responsibilities, here, only if your *whole* line consistently yields profitable productivity.

Four Profitability Standards

Your Department's human productivity will be consistently *profitable* only if it constantly meets *all four* of the following *standards:*

The "Q's"

1. Quantity

Your Department must consistently yield at least the minimum number of units set for it. For example: number of motors assembled, number of letters filed, number of vehicles dispatched, number of reports prepared, number of experiments completed.

No business activity is exempt from this requirement.

Quantify Everything

Every productivity responsibility or obligation can and must be quantified, even if the minimum number established is only *estimated*. Otherwise there would be no effective way to budget production, assembly, processing, etc.

Make No Exceptions

I've met many management men who believe that *their* operations are exceptions to this rule. But I've always been able to point out to each one of them that there was at least *one* valid criterion for quantifying his particular departmental productivity.

An Illustration

A case in point came up at one of the seminars I recently conducted. Here's a transcript of the discussion that took place.

> *Seminar Leader:* Every one of you can quantify your department's productivity.
>
> *Laboratory Head:* That doesn't apply to me. My department is constantly experimenting with chemicals in order to see whether we can come up with profitably-salable products. Our stock-in-trade is *creativity.* You can't measure *that* kind of human effort.
>
> *S.L.:* What's your annual laboratory budget?
>
> *L.H.:* About a million dollars.
>
> *S.L.:* Do you think that your company's president would be willing to wait until you've spent ten million dollars before you come up with one salable product?
>
> *L.H.:* Oh, no!
>
> *S.L.:* Five million dollars?
>
> *L.H.:* Well, no.
>
> *S.L.:* Two million dollars?
>
> *L.H.:* Yes, I think he'd be willing to do that.
>
> *S.L.:* Well, then, here's *your* quantification: You'd better come up with at least one profitably-salable product every two years, or you're not meeting your responsibilities the way your president wants you to.

2. Quality

Here's an example of how *effective* quality standards can be in the face of obstacles which seem to be immovable.

Ed Fuller was Quality Control Manager for a paperboard manufacturing company. He complained to me that he couldn't solve one particular problem common to his various assembly-line areas. Here was the typical setup.

The Workflow

The machines took the raw materials in at one end, mixed them properly, converted the mixture into paperboard and turned the finished product out at the other end. There were eight men on each machine, each one stationed at a different point on the long production line.

Each man was supposed to perform a specific, minor operation during the material's flow past him on the conveyor. But his chief function was to make sure that the mixture was even, as it passed him, so that the end-product would be free from lumps. Lumpy boards had to be rejected and re-worked.

Each machine had one foreman over its eight men.

The Problem

The difficulty was that when there *were* lumps, at the end of the line, the foremen claimed that they couldn't pinpoint the blame for careless-ness on any *one* of the eight men. The supervisors, of course, couldn't be physically present—at any one given moment—at *each* point of the long assembly line. And each worker stoutly denied that the fault was his.

The Solution

The problem was resolved as follows:

The foreman periodically stationed himself at such a point that he could see each finished board as it came off the machine. A quick visual inspection sufficed to show whether it was lumpy. If it was, he had it put on a special pile and asked each man, starting at the front of the machine and working down to the end, whether the mix had been uneven as it passed him.

If no one admitted that it had, the foreman blamed the man at the end, who had, of course, no excuse. It didn't take long before the men agreed among themselves to be more careful. The paperboard got no lumps, neither did the men.

Emphasize Quality

You must see to it that *every unit, of the desired quantity produced, is turned out with at least the minimum quality* called for by established standards.

Quantity is important to profit. But no unit of product or service, yielded by any employee of a company, makes a profitable contribution to over-all profitable productivity unless it has the *quality* essential to cus-tomer acceptance.

Quantify Quality

You must do everything in your power to *quantify* even your *quality* standards. Here, too, you may be able only to *estimate* the numerical value of the quality you insist on. But *quantify* quality you must, or your insist-ence on quality standards may be unenforceable.

Here are some examples of how you can *quantify* quality standards:

- Number of millimeters of tolerance.
- Percentage of presence of a particular chemical in the total mix.
- Number of erasures noticeable on a finished letter.
- Percentage of impurities in the finished product.
- Number of customer complaints about the service of a particular employee.

The "T"

3. Time

Your responsibility for the *time* standard in profitable productivity is illustrated by the case of an R and D Superintendent I've worked with.

Every prototype he's asked to develop is absolutely perfect in every respect, exactly the way it was called for. The only trouble is, it takes him twice as long to develop it as the carefully planned schedule estimates it *should* take.

Other Examples

- The Shipping Department Head who gets all the orders out properly, but always a week behind promised date.
- The Advertising Manager who sends every salesman copies of all ads—*after* these have appeared in the media.
- The Station Master who has a perfectly marvelous system for train information but can't get it to the passengers sufficiently in advance of their needs.

No Excuses

You may remember the story of the faithful, conscientious supervisor who'd never once been late in all the twenty years of his employment with the company.

One Sunday evening his daughter was married, and he didn't get to sleep until Monday, 4 A.M.

He awoke with a start, looked at the clock, and was distressed to see that it was 11. He dressed quickly and, on his way to the plant, rationalized to himself that he was entitled to be late at least one day in twenty years.

When he got there his boss began to bawl him out; whereupon he got real sore and shouted:

"How do you like that! For twenty years I wasn't late even once. Here I come in only a few hours late, and I get the dressing down of my life!"

"Never mind the few hours," retorted his boss. "Where were you all day Monday, Tuesday and Wednesday?"

Relate Time to Quantity and Quality

You must complete not only according to strict *quality* standards, but also *within the time called for.*

Prevent Unnecessary Time Costs

Delays in the completion of satisfactory work give rise to *at least* the following non-productive, or less than profitably productive, situations:

- More manpower is used than absolutely necessary, costing more money than can be profitably allocated.
- Space, machinery, equipment, utilities, parts and tools used on one job, for a longer period of time than necessary, prevent the *optimum number* of jobs from being completed.
- One slow operation can easily cause other operations to be delayed.
- Customers can become dissatisfied with delivery timing.

The "C"

4. Cost

Your fourth profitable-productivity responsibility is to yield the quantity and quality called for, at the time required, *at the lowest possible cost.*

In many of the companies where I've done consulting work, I've looked around at the people and things involved in the activities of the business.

- I've found people doing less than they're capable of.
- I've found some people doing little or nothing.
- I've found two people, each doing the same thing, perhaps without knowing it, where only one of them should have been doing it.
- I've found people spending too much time on the phone or in personal conversations.
- I've found machinery breaking down because of lack of preventive maintenance.
- I've found accidents occurring which could have been prevented.
- I've found end-products rejected which could have been manufactured so as to be perfectly acceptable.

Pinpoint Costs

The elements of *quantity, quality* and *time* which I've discussed above have, of course, an important impact on the *costs* of production. But there can be *additional* costs which are not called for. If these are permitted to arise, productivity becomes that much less profitable.

You must keep *all* costs (operations, manufacturing, R and D, etc.) as low as possible, consistent with productivity requirements.

See for Yourself

The self-test given below will help you evaluate the degree to which you are aware of your need for careful cost control, and the degree to which you are doing all that you can to exercise such control.

Elements of cost for which I am responsible	Am I doing everything possible to keep those costs as low as they should be?	
	Yes	*No*
1. The productive use, maintenance and repair of the grounds, buildings and/or space occupied by my subordinates and myself.		
2. The machinery, equipment and/or tools for which I am responsible.		
3. The utilities for whose use I am responsible.		
4. The materials and/or supplies for which I am responsible.		
5. The people (including myself) for whose productivity I am responsible.		
6. The Company money which I am authorized to spend.		
7. The productive use of time under my control.		
8. The customer-acceptability of finished products, services or other results of my line's productivity.		
9. Manpower retention.		
10. Regularity and punctuality of attendance at work by my line.		

Try This Experiment

Starting the first business day of your next full week, be conscious of everything you do each day. Ask yourself whether it's costing the company more than it should. If the answer is *yes,* fill in the chart on page 132.

Activity over which I have control	Areas where it is costing the company more than it should	What I can do to eliminate the unnecessary cost

Continue the Experiment

If the above exercise proves useful to you, use the form on a continuing basis, until it's no longer necessary to do so. And you might want to ask your subordinate management people to follow the same procedure.

Of course, you'll want to do something remedial—as soon as possible —in the areas of excessive cost which you put on the chart.

PROVIDE FOR SAFETY FIRST

In hundreds of management seminars I've conducted, I've asked this question: "What do you consider the most important criteria of successful productivity?" I've gotten many different answers, most of them absolutely correct. The one answer which I seldom get, however, is "Safety."

Now, I know that all the participants were fully aware of the importance of safety to their responsibilities. But what surprises me is that they don't uniformly come up with *safety* as the *first* answer to my question.

And why am I surprised? Because everywhere you go you hear and see the expression: "Safety First."

Put first what is first.

This illustrates the tendency of many people to know all the clichés and promptly push them down into their unconscious minds.

Safety Is Your Concern

You will agree that:

• The setting up and pursuit of safety standards for your entire subordinate line, in all of their activities, is your Number One Responsibility. You must undertake this consciously and carefully, and follow up on the degree to which your people fulfill the requirements set.

• You must pay this kind of attention to safety even if, at any one moment, company profit might suffer as a result. Appropriate safety regulations and programs—neither more nor less than absolutely necessary —must be established and followed regardless of their impact on profitable productivity.

• Of course, a good safety program, properly followed, is bound to *enhance* profit.

Keep Your House in Order

You realize, of course, that housekeeping is a necessary adjunct to safety. What do *you* do to improve this aspect of your operations?

One Plant's Gimmick

In one of my client plants the Industrial Relations Manager instituted a program of effective motivation for good housekeeping.

He had taken a broom and painted a face on the upper portion of the stick. About midway down he'd tied an apron. The broom had then been fitted to a sturdy stand, at the top of which appeared a placard with the broom's name: *Henry.*

Every week the Industrial Relations Manager and the Production Chief visited each department and decided which one was the sloppiest.

For the entire week following, *Henry* was stationed at the entranceway to that department.

Recognize the Importance of Good Housekeeping

Not only does good housekeeping contribute to safety; it is also a justifiable goal in itself.

- It makes for greater and better productivity.
- It helps reduce waste.
- It has a positive effect on morale.
- It's important when outsiders come to visit the company's facilities.

Safety and Housekeeping—Both First

While you're seeing to it that your subordinates get the production out *safely,* it's easy to make sure they understand their housekeeping responsibilities as well. Follow up on them to decide whether they're eligible for *Henry.*

KEEP MORALE HIGH

While making every effort to promote profitable productivity, pay careful attention to the state of morale among your men. Here's an example of what can result if you don't.

The Case of the Rush Order

It happened at an aluminum plant.

The Sales Manager had just told the Production Head about a new order for half a million dollars' worth of aluminum ingots. They had to be delivered in two weeks if the customer was to be held to his part of the deal.

The Production Head was vitally interested in company profits and hastily called together the appropriate Department Heads to plan to fill the order.

When one of his subordinates pointed out that the sudden addition of this new work load to existing schedules would cause undesirable operational upsets, the chief production man said he couldn't help that. The order had to go out on time.

Go out it did. And so did two very valuable members of production management. They'd had too much of this kind of company practice. They could no longer take the repeated disruption of normal, orderly planning and implementation which exceeded the demands of reasonableness and flexibility.

Pay Attention to Morale

You must avoid damaging the morale of your subordinates. Don't insist on frequent and sudden changes in plans.

Five Keys to Promoting Morale

1. As far as possible, don't issue orders the last minute.

2. If a new need arises which you think is an emergency or a crisis, put your finger to your temple, rather than on the "panic button." Ask yourself whether that new requirement couldn't really wait.

3. Keep the number of times when you violently and suddenly disrupt schedules to an absolute minimum.

4. If you *must* occasionally get an unexpected job done right away, try to assign the new burdens to those men who can most readily absorb the shock of changes in orders. Try to minimize the undesirable physical, mental and emotional overtones of rush productivity.

5. Explain to those involved *why* you must make the unexpected change. Apologize to them for the disruption. Promise them you'll try to avoid this in future. Help them adjust their present schedules to accommodate the new one. And thank them for their readiness to cooperate.

WEIGH PLUSES AGAINST MINUSES

It's good management to get the work out when an emergency arises. But why kill the goose . . . ? Before asking for efforts above and beyond the call, it might be wise to consider whether the harmful effects of that request may not be greater than the benefits that could be derived from meeting the new demands.

SUCCESS CAPSULE NUMBER NINE

In this *Success Factor* I've talked about your responsibility for making productivity profitable.

1. Every level of management has its own important part to play in assuring company profit.

2. But the major function of management *on* any level and *through* levels, is to assure profitable productivity by *Non-Management*.

3. Company profit will be continuously satisfactory only if the products or services to be sold are produced or created with the proper balance between operation *costs* and operation *results*.

4. Everything that goes on in your Department costs the company money. The goal must be to engage in only those activities whose cost can be justified in the overall productivity process.

5. You are responsible for your subordinates' continuously-profitable productivity. This will come about only if they consistently yield results which adhere closely to specifications in these four areas:

   a. The *quantity* of units turned out.
   b. The *quality* of each of those units, quantified as far as possible.
   c. The *time* within which they are turned out.
   d. The *cost* of this productivity.

6. While assuring maximum, human, profitable productivity, pay careful attention to the important considerations of safety and housekeeping.

7. Don't let a sudden conviction that a change is necessary in orders or plans—because of an emergency or a crisis—damage the morale or the continued effectiveness of your subordinates.

How You Can
Make Productivity
Profitable

This *Success Factor* relates to the techniques you can use to assure the highest degree of continuing profitability from your department's productivity.

CHANNEL YOUR MEN'S EFFORTS

Your success in achieving the kind of profitable productivity you want depends in large measure on the efforts and results of your subordinates. You have no problem getting *yourself* to do your best and most all of the time. But you must get your *subordinates* to exert themselves in the same way.

You can accomplish this only if, to begin with, you know what goes on in your subordinates' minds. Then you can decide what you have to do to get them to think and act as *you* want them to. And, having decided, you're then in a position to do something about it.

Here are some of the typical kinds of situations I'm referring to:

Portrait Number One

Perry Raven is a hard-working, conscientious Regional Manager for an Automotive Leasing Company. He has seven District Managers reporting directly to him. Each one of them has a geographical territory over which he has complete and exclusive profit authority, responsibility and accountability.

Perry knows no limits of hours, effort or energy. But business isn't so hot.

Perry assigns quotas to his subordinates. Then he buries himself in a mass of paperwork, which always seems to be waiting for him in his office. Some of his managers perform according to standards which Perry would himself have set. The others do not.

Portrait Number Two

Arnold Silver is Product Manager for detergents in a laundry-supply manufacturing house. Arnold spends only one day a week in his office. The rest of the time he's either in other people's offices, or out in the plant, or visiting customers to check on their satisfaction with his products.

"Create" a Man

Suppose you were designing a "human machine," expected to yield consistently certain specific products or services, to your entire satisfaction. What housing, parts, gears, dies, etc., would you put into that machine?

My experience has convinced me that unless you construct this "mechanism" according to certain definite specifications, it won't work the way you want it to.

Obey Laws of "Human Physics"

Just as a mechanical device will function only if it follows the unbreakable laws of physics, so will a "human machine" act properly only if it follows the "unbreakable laws" of psychology.

Managers who know the complicated principles of industrial technology wouldn't dream of expecting a machine to produce what it's supposed to if one of the basic laws of mechanics or electricity were violated. Yet many of these same executives fail to realize that profitable human productivity is dependent on certain unavoidable "laws" of human behavior.

ANALYZE YOUR MEN

Many management people unconsciously or automatically do and say the right things in order to get the human results they want. But many others don't. See where you belong in this categorization. Consider the following points:

1. *Factors in Performance*

A human being's job performance is the result of several factors, all interacting at the same time. Among these are:

    a. *Conscious decisions* followed by conscious thoughts, statements and/or actions.

FOR EXAMPLE: I decide to experiment with specific chemicals in order to see whether I can come up with a pigment which will better meet my customer's needs. I sit down and concentrate on the manipulations and thinking necessary to reach my goal. Everything I do is the result of my conscious determination to do it.

    b. *Unconscious reactions* leading to overt actions or statements.

FOR EXAMPLE: Yesterday my boss gave me a problem to work on, involving a more efficient materials-handling system for one of the operations in our department. At the time, I was busy on a previously-assigned task, and postponed my attention to the new problem until today. But, while I was continuing my work on the previous assignment, an idea suddenly came to me which I had not intended to bring up in my mind. I immediately made a written note of the idea, put it aside, and consulted it today.

    c. *Automatic responses* to internal or external stimuli.

FOR EXAMPLE: One of my colleagues, with whom I have a staff relationship, asked me to help him on a project for which he was responsible. Without thinking about it, I immediately felt a dislike for the task. Fortunately, I promised to help him. When he had left me, I forced myself to analyze why I had reacted that way. I realized that I had felt that he had spoken to me in a superior manner about his responsibility, and that I had resented his attitude. Without thinking, at least consciously, I had transferred my reaction regarding *him* to the idea that he had advanced, which was really a good one.

2. *Results*

You must make sure that your subordinates' efforts and energies are directed toward specific, desired results.

3. *Similarities and Differences*

Every human being shares certain reactions and habits with all other human beings. But every human being has many characteristics and reactions to specific situations which are different from those of the next fellow.

4. *Proper Assumptions*

You must not assume that your *own* reactions or actions are necessarily the same as those of your subordinates.

5. *Judgment of Your Men*

You must know your subordinates so well that you can judge how best to channel their individual characteristics. But, since each one of them has so many traits and reactions in common with all the others, the more you know about these *common* characteristics the better you'll be able to direct your men toward desired results.

It is these *common* characteristics that I'll now discuss.

CAPITALIZE ON COMMON HUMAN TRAITS

My contacts with thousands of management men lead me to the following firm conclusions.

A Guarantee of Profitable Productivity

Your people will consistently yield the kind of profitable productivity you want from them *only* if they constantly go through *certain* specific experiences, to be named herewith.

SEQUENCE OF THOSE EXPERIENCES

If your men are to yield consistently satisfactory productivity they should probably be exposed to those experiences in the exact sequence in which I present them.

TOTALITY OF THOSE EXPERIENCES

The omission of *any one* of those experiences can easily lead to less than desirable productivity.

ASSURANCE OF SUCCESS

The proper administration of *all* those experiences is *bound* to lead to success.

YOU MUST START IT

You must take the initiative to make sure that your subordinates live through all those experiences properly.

Now let's take up these experiences, one at a time.

TELL THEM WHAT YOU WANT

Many managers say that there are times when they just can't understand why some of their subordinates didn't do what they were supposed to do.

Try This Out

Ask one of your subordinates to tell you what he's working on at a particular time. See how closely his explanation comes to what you think you'd told him before he got started on it.

I've done this on a number of occasions, only to realize that somewhere along the line I'd failed to make my point. As a result of this I've learned to be much more exact in my instructions to people, and in my followup on the extent to which they understood me.

A Case in Point

As I sat listening to a Chief Security Officer conducting a meeting of his Guard Supervisors, I couldn't help realizing that he wasn't getting his message across. He wanted to make it plain to them that they were to tell their guards that there were to be absolutely no exceptions to the rule that all people had to show I.D. cards before being admitted to the plant. Here's the language he used:

"Even if a guard knows the man to be who his I.D. card says he is, he's to look at the I.D. card before he lets him in."

The next day it was discovered that an employee who had been fired that morning had been admitted to the plant by a guard. That employee had no reason for being there at that time. Investigation revealed that the guard hadn't consulted the daily list of lapsed I.D. cards before stopping that employee.

Who Was to Blame?

Was this the guard's fault? Perhaps. But let's look again at the instructions quoted above. Why didn't the speaker tell his supervisors to talk to their guards about the importance of consulting that list? Did he take it for granted that the guards *knew* that they had to do this? If so, why didn't he take it for granted also that they knew that they had to look at all cards?

THREE GOLDEN RULES

Here are three guides to success in telling your men what you want of them.

1. *Plan*

Before assigning any specific responsibilities to an immediate subordinate, think through and plan very carefully what you really want him to do, and the results you expect.

2. *Communicate Effectively*

Make sure to *communicate effectively* to your subordinates what you want them to do, and the exact nature of the results you expect.

3. *Follow Up*

Take all the steps necessary to assure that they undertake and continue this assignment successfully.

TRAIN YOUR PEOPLE WELL

Try this experiment.

Walk about among your subordinates, on all levels. See whether any of them are floundering in their work. Are some of them employing techniques less efficient than the best available? Is any time being wasted in experiments involving methods where you yourself already know the most effective approaches?

An Illustration

The month is November. The occasion is the company's annual evaluation review of all its employees.

The Superintendent of Production is worried that his foremen will again administer the review with the same old deficiency.

It seems that every year they rate the majority, if not all, of their men as "average" in every trait on the evaluation form. The superintendent has urged them again and again not to meet this evaluation responsibility so meaninglessly. And they've always understood what he meant. But he's never told them *how* to avoid the "average" trap.

A PLAUSIBLE METHOD

That was the situation when he asked me to meet with all of his foremen in groups of twenty, to try to solve this problem.

In each group I found that all the men really understood what the boss wanted. But they insisted that most of their men *were* average. They couldn't, therefore, see how they could avoid *reporting* that fact.

Of course, it didn't take me long to discover that:

• The evaluation form could do with some improvement.

• The foremen didn't want to take the extra trouble necessary to distinguish, among their men, between those who were superior and those who were inferior.

THE APPROACH

I resolved to take up with the superintendent, later, my suggestions for improving the form. But in the meantime, I decided to help the foremen break the impasse on "average" men.

I asked each group whether they believed there was such a thing as an "average man." Most said *yes*. I then conducted the following exercise.

GROUPING THE MEN

On the chalkboard was a list of the ten qualities on which they were supposed to rate their men. I asked them to get up and stand in the rear of the room. Then I suggested that each foreman mentally evaluate *himself* with reference to each of those traits.

I divided the room into three sections. The table to my left was designated "Below Average." The one in the center was labelled "Average." The one to my right I called "Above Average."

MOVING THEM ABOUT

I asked each man to sit down at that table which represented his own evaluation of himself with respect to the first quality. I then asked them to rearrange themselves or stay at the same table, according to how they evaluated themselves with respect to each successive trait.

After the tenth evaluation I asked how many of them had remained seated at the "Average" table for all ten traits; for nine; for eight; and so on.

In this way I was able to prove to them that it was impossible to evaluate any single group of men as "average" in *all* the traits on a representative listing.

ADD THE HOW TO THE WHAT

The superintendent had made perfectly clear to his foremen *what* they were to do. But he hadn't shown them *how* to accomplish this. He had left them to their own devices. And this resulted in their following the pattern common to all such evaluation procedures.

Three Steps in Training

1. After explaining to your men *exactly* what you expect of them, ask yourself whether they really know *how* most effectively to do what you've asked of them.

2. If you're not entirely sure that they do know how, or you're quite sure that they don't, explain the *how* to them *before* they start on the assigned tasks.

3. Check up on their performance before they go too deeply into the activity, to see whether your original explanation was adequate. If it seems not to have been, give them additional or different information.

GIVE THEM THE TOOLS THEY NEED

They tell the story of the man who had ordered soup in a restaurant. After it was served he beckoned to the waiter and engaged him in the following conversation:

The Patron: Please taste this soup.
The Waiter: Sir, if there's anything wrong with it, I'll be glad to take it back and bring you another plateful.
The Patron: Just taste the soup, please.
The Waiter: I'm sorry, sir, but I'm not allowed to do that.
The Patron: I insist. I want you to taste the soup.
The Waiter: Oh, all right. . . . But, where's the spoon?
The Patron: Aha!

Take the Third Step

Once you have adequately explained to your subordinates *what* you expect of them, and *how* they can do it effectively, you must be sure to see to it that they have all the facilities they need for carrying your instructions out successfully.

Whose Duty Is It?

But, you may say, isn't that *their* obligation?

Yes, but one key to good management is never to take *anything* for granted.

Suppose I assume that my subordinates are big boys, and that they know enough to ask me for anything they need that they run out of. I know from experience what this assumption will lead to.

Haven't you found that some people—even in the management ranks —will, if they need a particular object, simply wait until it's handed to them?

If they don't have a particular thing they need   and   they don't ask me for it   and   I don't think to find out early enough whether they need it

the assigned work won't get done on time or the way I want it done.

So, more important than finding out who's to blame is avoiding the need for that inquiry.

An Example

Ray Cutler was Chief Chemical Engineer in a paint factory. He was hot on the trail of a new formula which he'd been working out with R and D. In order to test the feasibility of the new process, Ray asked one of his subordinate supervisors, Allan Meadows, to assign several of his chemists to some necessary laboratory tests.

THE PLANNING STAGE

Allan knew exactly what Ray wanted, and was quite capable of carrying out the assignment. When he began to plan the allocation of tasks to the men he'd selected, he discovered that there was a shortage of one of the major pigments involved in the tests. Only Ray was authorized to make this material available.

Allan was a generally good man on the job, and his work attitudes were satisfactory. But he was very busy with tasks which had been assigned to him weeks before.

A POOR DECISION

When he saw that he couldn't perform the experiment in the exact way that Ray had specified because he lacked those pigments, he decided not to bother Ray, whom he knew to be very busy. He thought he could conduct the experiment with fewer people and fewer chemicals.

TOO LATE

Ray didn't discover this until a day after Allan had gotten started. Because of the requirements that Ray had set for the probe, he couldn't accept the work that Allan had begun. Ray had to arrange to deliver the required materials to Allan, in the quantities called for. But what had already been done was wasted.

A Better Way

An outstanding management man of my acquaintance told me that he learned his lesson about this kind of situation after he'd been careless early in his employment with his present company.

THE DELEGATION STEP

He'd delegated a very important new job to four of his immediate subordinates. Each one was supposed to have his mechanics perform specific functions related to the assembly of the item involved, and pass the unit on. Each subordinate understood exactly what his role was to be, and was fully capable of satisfactorily turning out the work assigned to him.

A Problem

The only trouble was that there weren't enough mechanics to go around, and two of the subordinates assumed that they'd get the help they needed whenever their boss was ready to provide it. So they put the work aside until they could get this help.

The Boss's Neglect

Of course, they should have taken the initiative and told the boss about their manpower needs. But they didn't. He found out about it after two days of delay, a delay which caused the whole assembly to fall behind in a tight schedule.

FOUR GUIDEPOSTS TO ASSURE RESULTS

1. When you plan the delegation of responsibility for a particular job, pay careful attention to the people, places, things and/or money necessary to assure its successful completion.

2. Make an inventory of what's needed, as against what's available. If you don't have all the information necessary for this inventory, get it.

On page 147 is a form which you might find helpful in your own facilities-planning.

3. As you explain assignments to your subordinates, make sure that they:

—Know exactly what facilities they'll need.

—Realize that they have what they need, to the extent that they do have it.

—Know how, when and where to get anything else that they need.

4. Check up periodically, as the work progresses, to make sure that the work is not being delayed, or improperly done, because of lack of facilities—or because of a mistaken impression that facilities are lacking.

Be Thorough

Here's a checklist of some of the "facilities" you may need to provide to your subordinates:

- Enough people of the right kind at the right time.
- Suitable and sufficient space of the right kind.
- A sufficient flow of utilities of the right kind.
- Enough machinery and/or equipment of the right kind, in proper condition, and available when and where needed.
- A sufficient supply of the tools, parts, materials or supplies of the right kinds, in proper condition and available when and where needed.

Assignment involved				
Segment of the assignment	Subordinate responsible for this segment	Facilities involved	When and where needed	Availability situation

Get the Best Out of Your Men

One of the greatest managers I ever knew, Larry Clark, told me of an experience he'd had with one of his immediate subordinates, Bernie Hammer.

Larry had just succeeded in having Bernie assigned to his department. This represented a step up for Bernie.

The first assignment Larry gave Bernie was to carry out an important work-sampling job in one of the plants. Bernie was familiar with the operation involved and knew the techniques required for his assignment.

Larry explained to Bernie exactly what he wanted done, and Bernie completely understood what was expected of him.

UNSATISFACTORY RESULTS

When Bernie turned in to Larry the results of his survey, it was apparent that they were not sufficiently representative of the daily operations in that plant to be meaningful. Larry asked for Bernie's worksheets and examined them. This revealed that Bernie had taken an insufficient sampling in every case.

THE REASON WHY

Further questioning showed that Bernie didn't like to do this kind of work. It bored him. Result: He did a less competent job than he was really able to do.

THE MORAL OF THE STORY

Larry told me that he never again took it for granted that one of his subordinates would do an assigned task *well* just because he knew *how* to do it well. From then on Larry always made sure to find out whether the man would really apply himself to the job in the way he was supposed to.

Another Example

The same sort of thing happened in another company for which I did consulting work.

Hank Peters was Soft-Goods Merchandise Manager for a retail department store. On reading the advertisements of the local emporia he discovered that his major competitor was featuring a particular kind of sports shirt which he didn't recall seeing on the buying report of his man responsible for that item.

Hank felt that the sports shirt advertised by the other store was a natural for that season, and that his store should have advertised it, too.

WHY THERE WAS NO AD

He asked his Sports-Shirt Buyer why he hadn't included that particular item in his advertising plan. The reason given was that that kind of shirt was "too loud" and would therefore not appeal to their customers. Hence the Buyer hadn't even bought it.

Hank didn't have the same feeling about that shirt. As it happened, the competitive store sold large quantities of that particular number.

Hank made sure, thereafter, to instruct all of his Buyers about the pitfalls of personal reactions to merchandise as distinguished from careful customer research.

Get Willing Cooperation

Bear in mind that *it isn't enough* to explain to your subordinates *what* they are to do and *how* they are to do it. Nor is your job complete when you have provided them with all the facilities they need.

There is *one* more element which *must* be present if you're to get from them the desired kind of performance.

Consider These Five Conditions to Success

1. You have a right to expect your immediate subordinates consistently to do their best and their "most."
2. No man will reach this height unless he really *wants* to.
3. Some of your subordinates usually, if not always, really want to.
4. Others may want to only occasionally, or they may never really want to.
5. Regarding these last, *you* have a special responsibility: to induce them to *want* to do their best and most—all the time.

An Obstacle to Motivation

A Sales-Manager friend of mine was in charge of the profitable sale of his company's dog-food division. Business was not so good, and he wanted to find out why.

During a sales meeting he asked the men this question: "Why isn't our dog food moving the way our forecasts said it would?"

WHAT WAS THE ANSWER?

No one seemed to want to answer. Maybe they didn't really know. Finally one salesman volunteered an opinion.

"The dogs just don't like it."

"Why?" asked the Sales Manager.

"How do I know?" was the reply. "I don't speak Dog."

Know What Will Motivate Them

You're going to have to do and say the right things in order to get your men to *want* to do their best and most. But before you can accomplish this you must *know* the motivations to which they will respond.

Find out what will inspire most men, and see whether you need to adapt this to particular men.

Then you'll be able to motivate *all* your men to want to do a good job.

SUPERVISE EVERYTHING DELEGATED

I've known management men who think they've done all they have to when they've:

- Explained to their subordinates exactly what was expected of them.
- Made sure their subordinates knew how to do this satisfactorily.
- Seen to it that their people had all the facilities they needed to do the job well.
- Motivated them to exert themselves to their fullest and best capacities.

Don't go only as far as that point and then wait for something to happen. It's one thing to prime a man so he's all set to do the right thing. It's another to make sure he follows through the way you want him to.

To illustrate the importance of this last step, let me tell you about some specific situations I've observed firsthand.

The First Case

This involved a Marketing Services Manager who'd thoroughly explained to his Market Research Supervisor what information was needed about a new product, and when the results of the survey were due. There was no question about the supervisor's ability to carry out the instructions, and he had all the instrumentalities he needed for the investigation.

The Manager left the discussion convinced that he'd adequately motivated his subordinate, as he really had.

An Unwarranted Assumption

But the higher-level executive didn't think it necessary to check up on the lower-level man. He simply took it for granted that the job would be done—properly and on time.

The day after the deadline he'd previously set, the Marketing Services Manager asked his subordinate for the report. There was none. Another assignment, given to him before this one, had bogged down.

In his sincere desire to make his own decisions and solve his own problems, the Supervisor had postponed the new survey until he could wind up the pending job.

The Second Case

This one concerned Walter Berry. He was Manager of Dealer Relationships for an automobile manufacturer. Walter had a number of Regional Managers reporting to him. He complained to me one day that some of his men never seemed to visit *all* of their dealers within the prescribed visit cycle. He asked me to look into it.

RESULTS OF THE INVESTIGATION

Two or three of the laggards weren't properly motivated to cover their respective territories fully. But the others really meant to get around more. It was just that some unexpected problem always seemed to pop up at one or another of the dealer establishments. And the proper attention had to be paid to each situation, which took more time than had been allotted to it.

THE RECOMMENDATION

I advised Walter to make a more frequent check on his Regional Managers' whereabouts, and helped him set up a system for doing so. In this way, he could foresee some of the cases where *one* dealer might not be visited because *another* required more than the allotted time. Armed with this knowledge, Walter was able to readjust schedules and assignments, to meet emergencies and crises and to assure more thorough dealer coverage.

SUPERVISE AND FOLLOW UP

You should check up on all important, delegated tasks. Don't take it for granted that you can completely rely on a well-motivated subordinate. There's many a slip. . . .

Here's some sound advice for you:

- Set up and stick to a carefully-planned system for supervising the fulfillment of every significant task delegated to your immediate subordinates.
- Follow up on the results of your supervision.

SUCCESS CAPSULE NUMBER TEN

In this *Success Factor* I introduced the basic concepts of how to make sure, continuously, that your subordinates will yield desired results. Here is a chart which will recapitulate the whole idea briefly:

Your immediate subordinates will consistently give you the kind of profitable productivity you want from them only if they constantly:	*For you to be sure that they consistently meet those requirements, you must continually and effectively provide them with the corresponding:*
1. *Know* exactly *what* you expect of them.	1. Communications.
2. *Know how* to do this properly.	2. Training.
3. *Have* all the *facilities* (which they need in order to do it well): on time, at hand and in good condition.	3. Planning.
4. *Want* to do their best and their most.	4. Motivation.
5. *Do* what they should, exactly as they should do it.	5. Supervision and followup.

How You Can Keep Your Men Profitably Informed

This *Success Factor* deals with your responsibility to keep your subordinates constantly informed of *their* roles in helping *you* continue to contribute maximally and optimally to your company's profit. It also spells out for you how you can most effectively keep them so informed.

EMPHASIZE THE "RAA"

As you know, the three most important characteristics of a Manager are his:

- *R*esponsibility for his men and for other company assets assigned to him.
- *A*uthority to exercise and enforce those responsibilities.
- *A*ccountability to his boss for his *Success* in properly fulfilling his responsibilities and authority.

In all of your *own* work you must keep your "RAA" uppermost in your mind and in your activities.

Pass the "RAA" On

You know that you must *delegate* to your management subordinates the maximum possible amount of your own responsibilities, with corresponding authority. Now you must see to it that *they:*

- Know what constitutes *their* Responsibilities, Authority and Accountability.
- Know *how* to accomplish this most effectively.
- Actually carry this out successfully.

Accept the Necessity for Informing Your Subordinates

It's dangerous for a Manager to *assume* that his subordinates know exactly what's expected of them. Even if there's a chance that they *might* know, without being told, it's an unnecessary and unwise risk to take such awareness for granted.

Tell Them and Tell Them Again

The only safe way to be sure that your subordinates are properly informed of their duties is to tell them what these are. And tell them as often as advisable.

Subtlety and tact may be necessary in order to avoid offending them. But the effort must still be made. And this *must* include *what* they're supposed to do, and *when, where* and *how* to do it.

Realize the Importance of Communications

Management specialists have been talking and writing for many years about how to establish and maintain effective communications in business. Yet, the failure of executives to communicate effectively with each other and their subordinates, is still the Number One problem in most companies. That failure is perhaps most marked in the efforts of *superiors* to make plain to *subordinates* exactly what's expected of them.

Make Your Communications Successful

The first step is to realize fully how easy it is to *fail* in this responsibility. Then, it's relatively easy to *succeed* in it. Because, knowing the pitfalls, you will do what's necessary to prevent their applying in your situation. You will thus strengthen your communications to your subordinates.

Avoid This Pitfall

Take a complicated assignment. You understand quite easily exactly what it involves. Some of your men may have difficulty in following its various elements.

Don't rush through the explanation without checking on each step to make sure that your subordinates are with you up to that point.

An Illustrative Case

In an appliance-manufacturing company the Quality Control Manager was explaining a special job-shop order. Only a few minor changes were called for in the mix of the ingredients. The Quality Control Manager had those changes clearly in his mind.

He quickly ran through the new specs, without interruption. Then he asked the foremen whether they had any questions.

THEY DIDN'T GET IT

Some of them were so confused they didn't say anything. Others simply asked for a repetition of the whole explanation.

Fortunately, the Quality Control Manager finally realized that he'd better take it step by step. But this was after two full explanations.

Take the Necessary Time

You're often under pressure to get a job done quickly. But remember the old adage about *haste* making *waste*. If there's the slightest chance that a new explanation—or a further one—might help, make it. It's better to invest a little time in additional clarification than to waste time in re-doing rejects.

Another Illustration

The right kind of explanation is generally made by Phil Ransom. He's Manager of Division Offices of an insurance company.

Every time the home office changes a policy, Phil calls a meeting of his Division Supervisors. He distributes copies of the new policy. He asks them to read them through right there. He then asks whether they've noticed anything different in that policy from the preceding one.

This leads him to a discussion of the few differences, and he makes sure that all present fully grasp them.

Everyone has had an opportunity to participate in the conversation. No one feels that his time has been wasted. And all go away fully informed on how to incorporate the new policy into their responsibilities.

Check on Your Subordinates' RAA

The first thing to communicate to your subordinates is *their* "RAA," in general and for each one of their specific assignments. When you do so, be sure that they:

- *Know* exactly what you're talking about.
- *Understand* it exactly as you intend it.
- *Enthusiastically accept* their "RAA" as you have effectively communicated it to them.

Unless you do all of this—all the time *and* effectively—you have no right to:

—Expect entirely satisfactory performance from them.

—Blame them if anything goes wrong.

Analyze Your Current Communications Practices

Take fifteen minutes a day, every day for the next two weeks, to fill out the checklist on page 157.

Evaluate Your Performance

As each job, assigned according to the chart, is finished, evaluate your satisfaction with the results. To the extent that you are *not* entirely satisfied, see how you described your satisfaction or dissatisfaction with the communication that preceded the assignment.

Rate yourself on how effective you were in communicating the corresponding RAA to the men involved. Then determine to be more effective in future RAA communications.

Three Guideposts to Effective RAA Communications

1. Through periodic observation, analysis and conversations, evaluate the degree to which each of your immediate subordinates knows, understands and *enthusiastically* accepts his general RAA.

2. Every time you assign a new or different task to any one of them, ask yourself whether it's advisable to make any additional explanation of the *specific* RAA for that job. If you're in any doubt on this, find some subtle way to resolve it.

Statements like these can be helpful:

"Let's review what's involved here."

"I know you realize that. . . ."

Date	Time	Assignment given to	For each assignment I think that the man involved understands his RAA				
			Entirely satisfactorily	Almost, but not quite	Fairly well	Only so-so	Poorly

"Just to satisfy myself that I'm thinking along the same lines as you, let's. . . ."

3. Never consider that you've gotten the ball rolling effectively on a new assignment unless you're *absolutely* sure that the men involved are *entirely* clear on their RAA: both in general, and for the specific task involved.

INSIST ON ACCEPTABLE STANDARDS

You can effectively communicate to your subordinates exactly what you want them to do *only* if you talk in terms of *Standards. You* must know what standards—performance specifications—you want met by your people. And *they* must know the standards they're expected to meet.

Establish Your Norms

You must decide on and effectively communicate to your subordinates the *norms* for each job. These should range from maximum/optimum, through minimum acceptable, down to *not acceptable.*

Here are *Eight Steps to Desirable Norms:*

1. Study carefully, for every task, the standards of performance each man *can* achieve.

For example, how many tons of a certain grade of iron can a conscientious torchman really cut in one day?

2. Make up your own mind on the standards of performance you're willing to shoot for and/or accept.

3. Translate this into easily-recognizable, understandable and achievable units, expressed in *quantified* terms.

For example:

—A tolerance of so many millimeters.

—So many pages typed in one hour.

—No more than two rejects a day.

—At least so many joint calls by the District Sales Manager with each of his salesmen.

—At least so much dollar volume of business generated by an advertising campaign.

4. Let your subordinates know clearly and definitely what those units are, how they have been quantified and how the finished units will be measured.

5. Tell them plainly and positively that you expect them to reach the highest possible number of acceptable units.

6. Let them know that you simply cannot and will not accept anything that falls below those standards.

7. Follow up on their performance and check the results against those standards.

8. Let them know how they are doing and have done. And keep them strictly to the standards established—at least to the *minimum* standards established.

Quantify Your Standards

You must try to *quantify* your norms. To the extent that you do not, you'll find your standards less enforceable.

Quantify Quality

Don't fall into the trap of thinking that *quality* standards can't be *quantified. Every* kind of business task *can* be quantified, even if only on an estimated basis.

If you probe deeply enough you can come up with a workable unit of quantification for every criterion of profitable productivity. If only an *estimate* is possible, *that* will serve almost as well, as long as you always use the *same basis,* for your estimates, in all cases of the same kind.

It's always possible to find *some* valid way of giving a *number* to any element of performance, including *quality* considerations.

A Case in Point

The head of the laboratory of a pharmaceutical manufacturing company insisted that his department's efforts and results couldn't be quantified. *They* were creative people, who tried to discover marketable products from chemical experiments.

He was asked how many years he wanted to be allowed before coming up with at least one marketable product. At first he didn't know. But further probing revealed that he would agree to the number *two.*

This meant that *his* quantification was: He'd better come up with at least *one* marketable product in *two* years.

Further Examples of Quantification

Get into the habit of analyzing from a quantification standpoint all the different kinds of jobs you assign to your subordinates. You'll soon find that you can readily establish valid numerical standards for every task. Here are some examples of how easily this can be done:

| *Kinds of jobs to be delegated* | *Kinds of quantification possible* | | |
	Quantity and time standards	*Quality standards*	*Cost standards*
Supervising the mounting of a component on a housing	100 per hour	Exact position in center of housing; "give" of the component, in relation to the housing: 1 inch	7¢ per mounting
Watching gauges	A careful examination of each of fifteen gauges, each one to be looked at once every two hours	Readings must be exact 100% of the time; danger signals must be reported to the superintendent not later than 10 seconds after noted	Amount of waste attributable to faulty production after the gauge has recorded a danger signal
Supervising a bank's Receiving Tellers	Average number of depositors a single teller should be able to serve in an average day: 125	Number of errors in any one day not to exceed *two;* number of justified depositor complaints not to exceed one a year	Cost of hiring an additional teller needed because the number of depositors satisfactorily handled by a particular teller is below standard
Controlling a manufacturer's R and D activities	Average number of projects of a specific type successfully completed within a stated time: 3	Prototype must conform to specs 100%, all of the time	Degree of adherence to the budget

Try It Yourself

From now on, every time you plan assignments to your men, fill in a chart like the accompanying one:

Task to be assigned	RAA for this task to be assigned to	Standards to be communicated to him for completing the task		
		Quantity/ Time Standards	Quantified Quality Standards	Cost Standards

ASSURE SUCCESSFUL COMMUNICATION "IN-DEPTH"

You should carry out your communications not only to your immediate subordinates, but also, through them, all the way down your line.

Your first obligation, in this connection, is to convey effectively to your immediate subordinates *their* duty to *delegate* appropriate responsibilities and authority.

Assure Proper Re-Delegation

Here are *Four Reliable Rules* for the effective communication of *when* to re-delegate.

1. Plan your own delegation to include the areas of RAA you wish re-delegated.

2. The first time you communicate to an immediate subordinate a specific type of responsibility, make it absolutely clear to him whether:
   - You want him to do it himself or, preferably,
   - To delegate it to one or more of his own immediate subordinates.

Many Managers follow their natural inclination to do things by themselves. They then complain that they haven't enough time to supervise their men. Usually it develops that their superiors *never made it clear* to them that they were to *delegate* most of the things they had been doing themselves.

3. Every time you re-assign the same responsibility to an immediate subordinate, make sure that he fully understands that this is one of his re-delegable duties. If that is *not* to be the case, make sure that he fully understands this.

4. When you supervise your immediate subordinates, check up very carefully on their faithful fulfillment of their indicated duty to re-delegate.

BE EFFECTIVE ALL THE WAY DOWN YOUR LINE

Your second obligation for effective downward penetration of your responsibility is to make sure that your wishes are clearly understood and followed by *all* your subordinates, on whatever level.

Unless you do so, you may run into the problem that faced the Warehouse Superintendent of a Steel Service Center.

He had repeatedly told the General Foreman in charge of the various bays, that processing and shipping priorities given them *had* to be followed *strictly*.

Every one of them fully understood and agreed with this requirement. But some of the *foremen* who reported to them frequently disregarded those priorities.

This caused considerable loss to the company, resulting from customer dissatisfaction with the fulfillment of delivery promises.

Three Keys to Success

To accomplish effective communication in depth:

1. Convey *only* to your immediate subordinates anything you want done by your non-management people.

2. Make sure that your immediate subordinates understand that *they* must see to it that your instructions and standards are properly passed down through the various layers between them and non-management.

3. Make sure that your immediate subordinates know how to do this effectively.

An Illustration

Study for a moment this fragment of an organization chart.

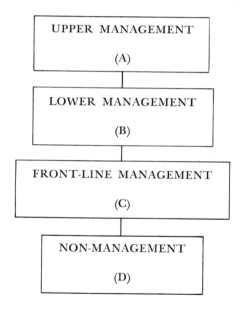

Now, assume that *you* are at the top of this chart (A), and that your subordinate line goes all the way down through the bottom of the chart.

Here's how you can effectively apply the concept of communication in depth, referring to that chart:

Anything that you want D to do you will, of course, communicate only to B.

For example, you might tell B that you want D to turn out 250 units a week, following prescribed, specific standards of quality, time, cost, safety and housekeeping.

How to Convey This Requirement

Your in-depth responsibility would be, then:
- To make sure that B fully understands
- That *he* is to communicate your instructions to C in such a way
- That C will communicate them to D in such a way
- That D will know exactly what's expected of *him*.

For the next few weeks as you get ready to assign new tasks intended for eventual non-management fulfillment to your immediate subordinates, use the worksheet on page 165.

You can, if you wish, use this kind of worksheet all the time, even after the trial run.

MAKE YOURSELF AVAILABLE

Now let's talk about another one of your important communication responsibilities.

You must be available to your subordinates for appropriate conversations with you, as sought by them.

Here are *Five Guidelines to the Best Policy* regarding when and how frequently you should accede to these requests for contacts.

1. Let your immediate subordinates know that they must feel free to come and see you on their own initiative, whenever they feel they should. (And, whenever you are about to go away from your desk, be sure to let someone in your office know exactly where you can be reached.) They must not, however, be too disappointed if they can't always take up as much of your time as they'd like to, *exactly when* they want to.

They May Have to Wait

Except in cases of real emergency, they must be prepared to wait until you can see them and spend all the time with them they need.

2. Instruct your men that, except as indicated just above, they should seek you out on their initiative *only when absolutely essential*. They must solve their own problems and make their own decisions.

If they feel they ought to see you, they should come prepared with

Task to be performed by non-management	Outline of how I can effectively explain the task to my immediate subordinates	Outline of how I can effectively guide them in their responsibility for carrying this message to non-management, through proper use of subordinate echelons of management	Time table and procedure for following up on the effectiveness of this communication while respecting echelons of management

a plan of action thought through as completely as possible, so that you can give them only that final assist which directs them properly. And the rule should be *fewer* than *more* visits.

3. Make it plain to them that when *you* want to see *them*—and this mustn't interfere too much with their need to be among their own men —they must make arrangements for adequate coverage in their absence, and come a-running.

4. You must go out into the "field" as often, and for as long a period of time, as possible.

5. You should let your subordinates know that you want them to come to see you every day, week or whenever you indicate. And, if there are to be in-between times when they are to come and see you, they should get as much advance notice as possible.

PREPARE YOUR REPLACEMENT

If you haven't already done so, begin a continuing program of evaluating your subordinates to see whether any of them could follow in your footsteps. And find one as soon as possible, so that when *you* are being considered for a higher position you have a sound replacement ready.

From every rung of the ladder you climb, always look down in order to select and prepare your successor, so that you are eligible for the next promotion. Don't let anyone above fear that you are indispensable in your current job.

Look Around All the Time

Don't be afraid of competition from your potential replacement. If a person reporting to you is better than you are yourself, he *deserves* to get a post you yourself aspire to. But such competition is extremely unlikely, for these two reasons:

• First of all, *you're* going to continue to grow, too. And you already have a head start over your subordinates.

• Secondly, as long as you're on your toes, your company isn't going to bypass you in favor of one of your subordinates.

Be Ready to Advance

To repeat, it's important to have someone who is ready and able to take your place when you become eligible for advancement. Your superior may even withhold a promotion from you if he's afraid that there is no one available to fill the position which you would vacate.

Don't Go Out on a Limb

You should not, of course, promise any of your subordinates that they are going to be recommended for promotion. But you should always have one or two of them in mind against the time when you may need a replacement. And then, too, you might be asked to recommend a candidate for a position on your own level in *another* department.

Help Your Men Advance

Even aside from the question of whether *you* will be advanced only if you can find a replacement for yourself, is the fact that you *owe* it to your company and to your subordinates to help them develop and grow to their maximum capacities.

Your company always needs good people to fill management vacancies. Why shouldn't these be *your* men? It's to *your* credit when *your* people are advanced.

And you owe it to them to help them rise in the company because anyone with ambition and ability deserves the opportunity to grow and qualify for suitable high openings.

A Plan of Action

Here's how you can meet this responsibility:

STEP NUMBER ONE: Let your immediate subordinates know that you are sincerely interested in their continued growth and development.

STEP NUMBER TWO: Constantly study and evaluate their ambitions, capabilities, attitudes and knowledge concerning their work and the company's activities.

STEP NUMBER THREE: Point out, to those you consider most promising, what they can do *by themselves* to *improve themselves*. And tell them you're always available to help them in this process of self-development.

STEP NUMBER FOUR: Give them opportunities for more study and practice most likely to help them grow. These opportunities can be either *within* the company or *outside* of it.

Make no promises of reward for their efforts. Simply inspire them to exert themselves for their own good. And, of course, don't spend any greater amount of company time or money on their development than your budget allows.

STEP NUMBER FIVE: Constantly evaluate their progress, and give additional help or stimulus wherever and whenever this might pay off.

STEP NUMBER SIX: When an opening comes up, for which any of your men might qualify, choose the man who, at that time, has attained the highest degree of development relative to that position. And then continue to encourage those who didn't qualify that time, to keep on trying.

BROADCAST YOUR CONTROL PLANS

There are two different schools of thought on the subject of whether to let your subordinates know what controls you will use.

The Cons

One group of people says: "I never tell my subordinates how I'm going to check up on them. In that way, they never know when the boom will fall, and will always do their best for fear that they'll be found out if they don't.

"If I told them *how* I was going to discover whether they were performing according to standards, they'd devise all kinds of ways of looking good on only those occasions when I was going to check up, and would goof off the rest of the time."

The Pros

The other group, with which I side, reasons as follows:

1. I want my immediate subordinates to do their very best and most —always.

2. I do everything in my power to get them to know and understand the standards of performance I've established for them.

3. I do my best to motivate them to meet these standards consistently.

4. I want them to know I have confidence in them, but I also want them to realize that I must and will supervise their work—carefully and constantly. And I want them to know why this is advisable and necessary.

5. I feel that if they know what controls I've set up and will exercise, they'll be able to understand more clearly the standards which are the basis for those controls.

6. I want them to realize that if they fail to pass the test of a particular control, they have only themselves to blame, and that they can't complain of surprise.

7. I know that if I keep them busy with delegated or assigned tasks, and that if they know that they'll be held to very high standards, they won't have *time* to goof off. And, if my controls are sufficiently compre-

hensive, every phase of their work will come under my careful and accurate scrutiny.

SUCCESS CAPSULE NUMBER ELEVEN

This *Success Factor* dealt with your responsibility for effectively communicating to your subordinates the tasks you want them to complete. It emphasized the following management responsibilities:

1. To make sure that your immediate subordinates *always* know *exactly* what you expect of them, fully understand what this involves and—without reservation—accept their responsibility to meet those requirements fully, accurately and on time.
2. To convey to them effectively the exact *standards* of performance which will consistently be expected of them.
3. To quantify every requirement passed on to them, even if the quantification is only on an estimated basis. This is so that they can measure their results—and, also, be held to account for them—on a fairly pinpointed basis.
4. To make sure that your management subordinates fully understand and willingly agree, that they are to *manage* their *own* subordinates, and *not do* the latter's work for them.
5. To let your subordinates know when and under what circumstances they should come and see you, while you urge them to meet their responsibilities on their own—with a minimum of consultation with you.
6. To help your subordinates—on a continuing basis—to develop themselves and grow, for their own as well as the company's benefit.
7. To be always on the lookout for people who can fill vacancies in higher positions, including your own.
8. To let your subordinates know, in advance, about the *controls* set up for measuring their performance and results.
9. To practice effective communications in depth. If your instructions and standards are intended, ultimately, for non-management, you must so convey them to your immediate subordinates that they will eventually reach their bottom "audience" exactly as you want them to.

   And almost immediately after completing a communication in depth you'll take steps to find out whether it "took" all the way down. If it didn't, you'll do everything necessary to overcome difficulties caused by any weak links in the communications chain.

How You Can

Communicate

Profitable ''How-To''

This *Success Factor* talks about training: by you for your people.

Once you've told a man *what* he must do, you must find out whether he knows *how* to do it properly. And if he doesn't, you must see to it that he effectively *learns* how.

TRAIN AT THE RIGHT MOMENT

One of the biggest stumbling blocks for Ted Burns was the great variety of specifications his job-shop assembly departments had to meet. He had very experienced foremen. But, when it came to a new kind of assembly job, one not quite like those they'd managed before, Ted was faced with a dilemma:

If he assumed that his men needed additional training in the basic techniques because of the differences between the new assignment and the old, and gave them such training, they squirmed impatiently at what they considered "old hat." On the other hand, if he *didn't* provide such training, some of them failed to direct the work properly, and production was characterized by excessive waste.

171

One Solution

One of my friends solved this kind of dilemma in a very simple way. He kept a record of every type of assignment he'd given to each of his subordinates. Then, before telling them about a new or different job he wanted them to undertake, he consulted his checklist. This helped him decide *when* to add *training* to his explanation of the new task.

You will want your men to know how to do their work well. But you don't want to train people who don't really need it. You could benefit by a simple, valid set of criteria for deciding whom to train, when to train him, and *in what* to train him. Here are some guidelines which may prove helpful.

RULE NUMBER ONE: Keep a continuing, up-to-date record of the types of assignments you've already given to your immediate subordinates. One possible form of checklist is presented on page 173.

RULE NUMBER TWO: Before you start explaining a new or additional assignment to a subordinate, consult this record. Come to a decision—based on the similarities or differences between assignments, the time elapsed since the last completion date, and his success at that time—on whether he should have additional training for the new assignment.

RULE NUMBER THREE: Plan your approach to the training aspect of your explanation of the assignment. Find a subtle way to make him accept your instruction without feeling belittled. Expressions like the following can be effective:

"As you know, . . ."

"Let's go over this again to be sure we both see it the same way."

"Please help me review this job so I don't leave anything out that I ought to tell you about."

RULE NUMBER FOUR: First tell him *what* he's supposed to do on the new assignment. Then guide him to knowing *how* he's supposed to accomplish it.

RULE NUMBER FIVE: Before indicating that he's to go ahead on the assignment, make sure he understands fully and accurately the techniques, methods, etc., that you've been explaining to him.

RULE NUMBER SIX: Check up periodically, especially soon after he gets started on the assignment, on whether he *really* understood your explanation. If you discover that he didn't, provide the necessary additional or different instruction.

RULE NUMBER SEVEN: Don't spend time giving training to anyone who doesn't really need it, whether for an entire assignment or for any part of it.

Subordinate's name	Type of assignments he's already completed successfully	Date of last successful completion of such assignment	Evaluation of his apparent knowledge of how to meet that assignment satisfactorily

TELL HIM THE RIGHT THINGS

Some Managers go all-out in explaining to their people how to carry out assignments. Others don't bother at all, taking it for granted that their men know exactly how to do what's being assigned. Somewhere in between lies the happy medium.

An Illustration

As I sat listening to a telephone company Customer Service Manager talking to his District Managers, I couldn't help but admire his approach to the training situation.

TECHNICAL PROBLEMS

He was explaining a new assignment to them. The company had recently introduced an innovation in the use of the telephone, and subscribers were just beginning to be faced with problems connected with the new setup.

The Manager was pointing out to those present that they'd have to make sure that their subordinate Service Supervisors properly guided the company people who were contacted by the customers. Involved in this guidance was a fairly comprehensive understanding of the technical aspects of the new service.

A REVIEW

The Manager reviewed with his men the way the system was supposed to work. He didn't go into any detailed explanation of the technology involved, but when he was finished they all understood enough about it to be able to pass on to their subordinates the necessary highlights of the new setup.

Ten Bases to Touch

When you explain *how* to carry out an assignment effectively, be sure to cover as many of these points as are applicable:

1. Special planning techniques involved in the new assignment.
2. Suggested approaches to the scheduling of manpower, space, machinery, equipment, etc.
3. Innovations which might be helpful in materials-handling.
4. Pertinent details on the technologies involved.
5. Intricacies of the processes in question.
6. Technical problems which may come up, and how best to solve them.
7. Details on testing and inspection procedure.

8. How to handle the necessary paperwork most efficiently.
9. Industrial-engineering aspects of the workflow.
10. How to make machine setups for the processes involved.

HOW TO SUCCEED AS A TRAINER

Some time ago a Manager told me he'd never been a good trainer, that he was not *then* a good one, and that he *never* expected to be one. When I asked him why he felt that way, he voiced that universal—and false—cliché: "Teachers are born, not made."

I finally succeeded in convincing him of these *Three Facts About Trainers:*

• Anyone intelligent enough to have risen to his present level in the company has all the inherent ability he needs in order to learn how to instruct others effectively.

• Nobody can continue to be responsible for the work of others unless he can—and does—effectively train them in their duties.

• There are definite techniques for training which anyone in his position can—and should—learn.

Here are *Ten Basic Principles* of effective training:

1. Always plan training sessions in advance, with a clear idea of *what's* going to be discussed, and *why* and *how* it's going to be discussed.

2. Have available, before starting, all the materials and equipment needed for the training session.

3. Have in mind a clear idea of your objective(s) for that session.

4. Start the session by stating that the purpose of that meeting (or of a particular portion of the meeting) is to go over with those present *how* to accomplish a new (or different) assignment.

5. State (or re-state) the assignment in question, and make sure, before proceeding any further, that they all fully and accurately understand what's involved.

6. Find, and start with, the most basic concept—related to the assignment—known to all those present, as a point of departure for your explanation.

7. Then introduce the first detail which they may not *all* know how to follow properly. Relate that detail to the basic concept already known to them, and explain the new point until you're satisfied they all understand it fully and correctly.

Ask questions wherever possible, so that you can tell whether or not they *do* understand the particular point involved. (A mere "yes" or "no" answer is not enough.) If you're not completely satisfied that they *do* understand it, try a different way to explain it until they do get it.

8. Summarize the point just made and take up the next one, in the same way as described above.

9. When you've made the last point, summarize the whole session, give them an opportunity to ask questions, and provide for followup on the training.

10. Check up on their real understanding of what you've explained: soon after the training session and frequently thereafter.

A Suggested Tool

You may want to use a "training-plan" form like that following.

New task

To whom assigned

General description of the subject matter of the instruction

Date, time and place of the instruction

Materials and/or equipment needed for the instruction

Estimated duration of the instruction session

Remarks to be made on opening the session

DETAILED PRESENTATION PLAN

Point to be made	*Questions and/or statements which can be used in developing the point*	*Audio-visual aids to be used*	*Summary, and tie-in with the next point to be made*

Final summary

_____

Arrangements for followup

_____

Evaluation of the training session

TRAIN IN DEPTH

As you know, every step you take in the management of your *immediate* subordinates must ultimately penetrate all the way down your line. Here is how this principle can apply to the *training* responsibility:

You will, of course, limit your own training efforts to your immediate subordinates, but you'll want to make sure, in your sessions with them, that they:

• Fully understand and agree that they must see to it that proper training goes from them all the way down their respective lines, through proper channels.

• Understand and agree that they can't consider their responsibility for this training properly met just because they've *told* their immediate subordinates about the need for in-depth training. (*They* must make sure that *their* immediate subordinates see to it that *their* immediate subordinates—and so on, right down through non-management—give and/or get all the instruction needed for the assignment.)

• See to it that *their* immediate subordinates—and so on, right through Front-Line Management—know *how* to train their respective subordinates effectively.

SUCCESS CAPSULE NUMBER TWELVE

This *Success Factor* has emphasized that you must make sure that your subordinates know *how* to meet their responsibilities to your entire satisfaction. You can take the steps necessary for such assurance, either *after* explaining a new assignment, or *as part of* the explanation.

In order to accomplish your objective you must:

1. Decide *who* needs *what* training or instruction.
2. Plan your training sessions well in advance of the actual time you're going to give the instruction.
3. Insist not only on complete *understanding* of how the job is to be done but also on full *agreement* that that's the way it *should* be done and *will* be done.
4. Check up, just as soon after the training session as possible—and as often thereafter as may be necessary, to see whether any additional instruction is called for.
5. Carry this training responsibility and activity *in depth* all the way down through Front-Line Management subordinates, until all non-management involved is properly instructed for the new job.

Maximize Your
People-Motivation

How You Can
Plan Successful
Motivation

This *Success Factor* talks about how you can get your people to *want* to do satisfactorily what they are supposed to do. It also presents some helpful techniques for succeeding in this objective.

PORTRAIT NUMBER ONE: Marv Block is a bright, knowledgeable, experienced Project Engineer. No one is keeping from him the things he needs for doing his job well. But he's consistently behind a schedule he fully understands and knows how to meet.

PORTRAIT NUMBER TWO: Rudy Chadwick has no problem getting started properly on his company's computer-programming schedule. But his programmers always manage to make at least one major—and avoidable —mistake.

PORTRAIT NUMBER THREE: Dave Wyman has all the people he needs, all of the right kind, for turning out a consistently-acceptable bottle top. But Dave's production costs frequently exceed a budget which he himself has previously suggested.

ANALYZE THESE SITUATIONS

What's happening here? What's going wrong? Is this kind of failure unavoidable? Let's see.

Know How Much You Can Expect

You've carefully planned the delegation of another job to one or more of your immediate subordinates. You've explained to those involved *exactly* what's expected of them, and they understand and accept this completely. They know *exactly* how to accomplish their tasks satisfactorily. They have *all* the facilities they need in order to fulfill them as called for.

Is anything missing?

A PROBLEM

An industrial psychologist once told me about a case he'd come across in one of his client companies.

The Assistant Manager of a large hotel was concerned about the excessive turnover in chambermaids. Investigation revealed that the women left mostly because the housekeeper seemed never to be satisfied with the way the rooms were made up. The Assistant Manager consulted my friend on this problem.

THE CAUSE

It didn't take long to learn that the housekeeper was setting standards of performance for her girls which were more exacting than the criteria she'd used in hiring them.

Be a Realist

Tone down your own perfectionist tendencies. At least, be ready to accept *less* from your subordinates than *you* are able to yield. Don't kid yourself about what you can *get,* as distinguished from what you *want.*

But if you refuse to accept less than what you want, just don't hire or keep anyone who falls short of your standards.

The only way I know of making a silk purse out of a sow's ear is to start with a silk sow.

Six Practical Policies

1. Set your standards—for taking on subordinates—as high as possible.
2. Look for people who come as close to those standards as possible.
3. Weigh the relative merits—and cost—of waiting longer (until you find the kinds of people you want) against the practical advisability of taking the best people you can get and trying to upgrade them.
4. Make the best selection from what's available, when decision can't be postponed.
5. Keep on looking for better people, and replace your marginal subordinates (by putting them into positions they *can* profitably fill) by those better people.
6. Study and find out the maximum/optimum *capacities* of the people you put into your subordinate line.

Be Practical

But bear in mind the following caution: While you should always try to get your people to yield the *most* and the *best* of which they are capable, *never expect more or better out of them than they can possibly do.* And it's no excuse that you didn't know that your men couldn't do any more or any better than you had hoped.

THE KEY TO MOTIVATION SUCCESS

Do everything in your power to get your subordinates to turn in results which consistently represent their best efforts, from both a quantitative and a qualitative standpoint.

An Example of Maximization

The story is told of the circus strong man whose side-show act consisted of cutting an orange in two and squeezing one half until it seemed impossible to get any more juice out of it. He would then offer $50 to anyone in the audience who got a single, additional drop of juice from what was left of the squeezed half.

In one town a slight, short man of about sixty-five years of age volunteered to meet the challenge. Accompanied by the snickers and sneers of the performer and the audience, he mounted the platform. He took the depleted fruit in his right hand and—*squeezed a cupful more of juice out of the rind.*

THE REASON WHY

When the winner had been duly applauded, amid the gasps of amazement, and had received his reward, the strong-man said to him:

"But tell me. How could you, who are so puny, get any more out of that orange half?"

"You see," replied the other, "I'm a professional fund-raiser for the United Community Appeal."

MAKE THEM WANT TO

I suggested to Jerry Martin, Program Director for a radio-TV broadcasting system, that he perform an experiment with his show producers. Here's how it went:

Each producer was to pay special attention to costs for one full week. At the end of that time, a report was to be turned in to Jerry. All that was required was the filling in of the blanks next to the pre-typed captions.

An Evaluation

I asked Jerry not to look at the reports until he had first made an educated guess on which producers would show the closest adherence to budget for that week.

Jerry's estimates were quite accurate. With only one exception he had predicted who would rate a high score and who a low.

And the criteria Jerry employed? The attitudes of his creative people toward so mundane a consideration as money—the Company's money, that is.

This ability to call shots right, which Jerry demonstrated, is not an exceptional one. Any seasoned Manager can be just as accurate in similar judgments.

EXAMPLE: A chain restaurant Commissary Manager who can tell you within a hundred dollars how much each restaurant manager will waste each week in unused provisions.

EXAMPLE: A Chief Designer who can predict which of his supervisors of sample-making will consistently turn out the largest number of well-made garments for display and promotion purposes.

Wanting Leads to Doing

Reputable industrial psychologists throughout the country have come to the conclusion, based on studies of thousands of executives in industrial and commercial establishments, that:

A person will consistently exert himself to his fullest and best capacity only if he really wants to.

I don't, of course, mean that the *desire* to put forth one's fullest and best exertion is enough in and of itself to assure that such exertion will be the result. Other factors may determine whether the *will* to expend the desired energy will bring about the actual effort.

But if you want any of your subordinates consistently to put forth their greatest and best efforts, someone or something must induce them really to want to make that kind of effort.

Move the Immovable Object

Some of my clients have reacted to the above statement by saying something like this:

"So what? Most people—certainly, most management people—are sincere, conscientious and loyal. They have a sense of fair play, and usually want to do the most and the best they can. And on those few occasions when they don't, there are reasons beyond their control for their lesser contributions."

My reply to them has always been: "Are you sure?"

Try This Experiment for a Week

1. Evaluate each one of your immediate subordinates along the lines suggested by the accompanying checklist.

Name	Date	Assignment		Degree to which I was satisfied with the results	If the preceding column indicates anything less than 100% satisfaction, why he failed to meet my expectations
		Nature	Date Due		

2. At the end of the week, make a careful analysis of your chart. Try to pinpoint *which* of your people failed to do *exactly* what you'd hoped because they *just didn't make that extra effort.*

An Unfortunate Situation

The fact is that many people simply do not *want,* at least some of the time, to work as hard or as well as they can.

Now don't get me wrong! I'm not advocating that anyone be asked to work constantly under pressure or tension. But a management man must realize that he's been put into his present position not only because he has special abilities, but also because he has special obligations.

The Goal

It's perfectly feasible for a man to try his darndest all the time, and still not overdo it. All I'm asking is that he *want* to give of his maximum/optimum abilities. *You* will be the only judge of how hard your men should actually work.

Competition in business today is so great that unless you consistently get the maximum quantity and quality of management and non-management productivity from your people you're just not going to be able to make the kind of profit contribution you want to.

Test Your Own Habits

- Do *you* ever feel like doing less than you're capable of?
- Are *you* occasionally tempted to "take it easy"?
- Do you turn the alarm off, once in a while, so you can get a few minutes' extra sleep?
- When was the last time that you visited with another executive for reasons a little beyond the business purposes of business-day contacts?
- Do any of your office phone conversations last a little longer than even *inter-personal relations* require?
- Do you sometimes take longer over lunch than business really calls for?

Set an Example

If you want your subordinates to give their all for "dear old Alma Mater," make sure not to be vulnerable to *their* complaint that *you* don't practice what you preach.

Five Basic Concepts
- Profitable company management requires tremendous competitive productivity.
- You've accepted the privileges of your position of your own accord. You therefore owe your company a maximum/optimum contribution to its success—on a continuing basis.
- The same is true of your subordinate management people.
- You *must* want to do your best—all the time, whether or not you enjoy that kind of exertion.
- The really smart executive learns to *enjoy* such maximum/optimum exertion, and to relax while engaging in it.

BE THE "IRRESISTIBLE FORCE"

This was told to me by the Chief Maintenance Engineer of a smelting and refining company:

"I've had Maintenance Crew Chiefs who always knew just what it took to get a job done properly and promptly, who had no problem getting their men started on, and keeping at the job. While I checked up on them from time to time, I could leave them pretty much alone, because I could always depend on them to do the best they could in each case.

"On the other hand, I've had other chiefs who had to be prodded all the time. They were good men. They knew their business, and they weren't exactly lazy. It's just that they had to have a fire lighted under them before they'd realize the situation was hot and required forceful action."

Distinguish Between Categories

You will, no doubt, agree that when it comes to the desire to do a good job there are two kinds of people. The two types must be separated out and handled differently.

KNOW WHO GETS UP HIS OWN STEAM

Companies are full of people who always want to do their best and their most, who don't need someone to fire them up. I call this kind of man a *self-motivator*.

An Outstanding Example

Mike Driscoll is Chief Design Engineer of an automotive-equipment manufacturing company. Mike has several groups of Design Engineers reporting to him, through their respective supervisors.

You'll find Mike at his desk every business day well before the others come in, doing all his planning before he's needed for his other duties. He moves about all day among his people, not spending too much or too little time with any of them. His lunch periods are long enough to permit him to eat properly; he doesn't hang around the cafeteria after he's finished his meal.

And Mike doesn't mind remaining in his office half an hour after the others have gone.

Mike's results are, in general, superior to those of his colleagues in other departments.

I asked Mike's boss what he had done to get Mike to function that way.

"Nothing," was the answer. "And nothing *has* to be done. Mike's a self-starter. He's just that way. He can't be any other way. I wish I had more like him."

Handle Self-Motivators Properly

There are many reasons why a man becomes and continues to be a self-motivator, but whatever the reasons, his boss has certain specific responsibilities toward him. Here they are:

1. Carefully observe your subordinates in order to find out which of them *are* self-motivators.
2. Let *them* know that *you* know that they are self-motivators and that you appreciate this.
3. Do whatever you can to compliment and/or reward them for being what they are and doing what they do.
4. Don't spend any time motivating them to do what they're already doing.
5. Keep on observing them and their work, just in case they *stop* being self-motivators, for whatever reason.
6. If they do stop, try to get them back on the previous track.
7. If you can't, treat them in the way I describe below for those who *aren't* self-motivators.

STOKE THE FIRES THAT NEED STOKING

One or two members of a Company's Management group may be the kind who simply don't get their own steam up, at least not all the time. I call such people *Non-Self-Motivators*. It isn't hard to spot them.

I think it's safe to say that a management man can be both of these two things at the same time:

Names of my immediate subordinates who are currently Self-Motivators	Names of my immediate subordinates who are currently not completely Self-Motivators	How much stimulus I must apply to those in the center column

- A non-self-starter;
- An individual capable of being *induced* to do his best.

Naturally, it would be preferable to have *only* self-motivators on your Management Team. But if one or two of your subordinates are well-qualified for their positions except that they won't give their all without an occasional or periodic push, I guess it's better to give them the necessary momentum than not have them at all.

Analyze Your Men

I think we all know management people who:

—Always complain they have more to do than they have time for.
—Have to be reminded about past-due reports.
—Are frequently behind in production schedules.
—Fail to pay proper attention to safety requirements.

If you'd like to make an inventory of your people, from a motivational point of view, the form on page 189 can be helpful.

Motivate the Non-Self-Motivators

Here are your responsibilities regarding your Non-Self-Motivators:

1. Know who they are, both the perpetual Non-Self-Motivators and those who are only temporarily so.
2. Find out *why* they aren't self-motivated, and whether they can be stimulated to join the group of "Self-Steam-Getter-Uppers."
3. Try to get them to become and stay Self-Motivators.
4. If or when you *can't* get them to join the other group, keep on providing the necessary *external* motivation.

SUCCESS CAPSULE NUMBER THIRTEEN

In this *Success Factor* I began a discussion of *motivation*. Here I talked about:

1. Finding out and knowing your subordinates' maximum/optimum capacities.
2. Setting as your goal getting them to exert themselves continually to their greatest and best capacities, along lines set down by you.
3. Realizing that your men will consistently do their best and most only if they really *want* to.
4. Finding out which of your men *always* want to do their best and most, and encouraging them to keep on that way.
5. Knowing which of them need outside stimuli to get them to want to do their best and most, and providing them with those stimuli.

How You Can
Get the Most
Out of Your Men

This *Success Factor* tells you *how* to motivate the people you *have to* motivate.

You must see to it that all of your subordinates constantly exert themselves to their fullest and best capacities, along lines you set down and effectively communicate to them. If you're not satisfied with a man's capacities, you may have to arrange to move him elsewhere—in or outside of your company. But if you let him stay in your department you've got to get him to work up to snuff all the time. This effort on your part is called *motivation*.

PREPARE THEM EFFECTIVELY FOR MOTIVATION

You *must* set the stage properly, before you motivate your men, or you're liable to waste much of your time in the process of getting results. Here's a re-statement of the basic principles and practices of sound scientific management which precede motivation:

Recapitulate

- You've effectively told your men exactly what you expect of them.
- You've effectively explained to them exactly how to do—to your entire satisfaction—what you've asked them to do.

191

- You've seen to it that they have all the facilities they need for the satisfactory completion of the work, the facilities being in good condition and on hand.

Now you—and they—are ready for the motivation process.

Analyze Your Men

The first step is to review your current separation of subordinates into the *Self-Motivators* and the *Non-Self-Motivators*. And, make sure that at the time of your motivation efforts, the division is accurate. Then, remember to apply to the *Self-Motivators* those few stimuli which may be necessary for them, but concentrate your motivation efforts on the *Non-Self-Motivators*.

Know What Moves Men

There are only four basic motivations which you can apply to your men to get the results you want:

1—Money.
2—Job security.
3—Psychic satisfactions.
4—Promotion (for the sake of promotion, aside from the question of more money).

These are listed in the *descending order* of their impact on people in business, in keeping with my own experience with thousands of men and women who work for a living.

MOTIVATE WITH MONEY

You *must* take full advantage of the effect of money on people's desire to do well what they've been engaged for. To do so requires that you achieve these results:

1. Forget the many misleading statements that money is not a prime motivator.
2. Learn to make the most effective use of the *fact* of money's motivational force.
3. Apply this motivation in the most effective way available to you.

Give "Money" Its Due

First, the "money isn't everything" theme.

Many conscientious and well-meaning individuals are convinced that "money" is not as strong in motivating people as are non-monetary stimuli.

Some of this thinking stems from "surveys" made for determining what motivates employees. One of these "studies" in particular merits detailed examination.

A Case in Point

The investigator went to many different companies. With top-management approval, he met with groups of employees on all levels. In every contact he announced that he wanted to know what motivated them to exert themselves to do a good job. He told them he would distribute a questionnaire to them for that purpose. Would they please fill it out and return it to him?

WHAT THEY WERE TO DO

The questionnaire had the following "instructions":

"Below is a list of twenty-five reasons why an employee might want to do a good job. Please put the number '1' in front of that reason which *you* consider the most important to you, the number '2' in front of the one of the next importance to you, and so on down the line."

The twenty-five reasons, arranged in random order, included expressions like: "Pride in accomplishment," "A pat on the back" (and all the other well-known psychic satisfactions), "Money," "Job security," and "Opportunities for promotion."

Note that the word "Money" was presented in just that bare way, without any qualifying expressions.

THERE'S MONEY AND THERE'S MONEY

In the great majority of responses, "money" was way down on the list of motivating factors. From this the investigator drew the conclusion, among others, that *money* was not an important motivating factor. Certainly, he said, it was not as important as the psychic satisfactions.

I contend—and my experience substantiates this—that the conclusion is mistaken. And I present here the flaw in the reasoning.

HOW MUCH MONEY?

The motivating factor was stated merely as *money*. Unconsciously, most people take it for granted that they'll be paid at least *some* money for the work they do. Therefore, when they see the word "money" on a questionnaire, they assume that it means "more money." If they put "money" (which can mean *whether they get paid at all*) low on their list because they interpret it as "more money," the conclusions drawn from this survey are not scientifically accurate.

Money as a Positive Motivation

My experience is that the following statements are universally applicable to employees on all levels:

1. To the extent that you can offer your subordinates more money for better results, you will find a great many people eager to qualify for this additional monetary reward. It is, of course, true that some will not be interested. For them we have other motivations, which will be discussed below.

2. *Everyone* will respond to the motivation of *money* (as such) if you put it to him properly and with the correct connotation.

See for Yourself

Try this experiment, with the approval of one of your immediate subordinates.

Ask one of his good men whether he'd be interested in qualifying for a higher position in the company. If he says *yes,* tell him this: "In your new job you'd have a very dignified title. You'd be treated with great respect and dignity. You'd get much more satisfaction out of that job than from your present one. You'd be eligible for still higher positions in the company.

"There's only one thing. At present you're earning X thousands of dollars a year. I can't give you any more money in your new position—ever. You'll earn less than all the others on your level. Some of your immediate subordinates will earn more than you."

Then ask him whether he's still interested in the promotion.

BE REALISTIC ABOUT MONEY

Here's how to use *money* as a motivation.

a. To the extent that it's possible in your company or department, let your subordinates know—through the proper channels—that the better the results, the greater the monetary reward.

b. When you engage a new subordinate, point out to him that his job calls for certain specific standards of performance. You are confident that he will always exert himself to his fullest and best capacity, and far exceed any of the minimum standards which must be set for marginal employees.

c. Whenever any one of your immediate subordinates begins to perform below what you consider minimum acceptable standards for his position, give him this:

Ten-Point Message:

1. Tell him that you're not satisfied with his efforts and his results.
2. Remind him that you've done everything in your power to guide and motivate him to do more—and better.
3. If you're in a position to do so, remind him that he can earn more money (either in his present position or by a promotion or transfer) if he shows that he deserves a recommendation for such an increase.
4. Tell him that he's getting his present salary *only* as compensation for doing his best—and most—*all the time.*
5. Point out to him that you can't justify continuing to pay him that amount if his attitudes toward his responsibilities are not on an acceptable level.
6. Assure him that you're willing to continue to help and guide him as much as you can, in his efforts to improve his results.
7. But let him know in no uncertain terms that if he continues to fall below your standards—of effort, exertion and results—he may find himself in another and lesser job. There his attitude toward his work will more closely approximate what the job calls for.
8. In extreme cases, tell him you may have to recommend that he be dismissed altogether.
9. Assure him that you'll be fair with him and will give him every opportunity to improve.
10. End your talk with him on a positive note by telling him you're confident that he'll *want* to do better, that he *can* do better and that he *will* do better.

Be Ready to Act

If, despite all your efforts, this man continues to do less than you deem acceptable, you may have to recommend his transfer, demotion or dismissal.

CAPITALIZE ON JOB SECURITY INTEREST

Now take the man who doesn't respond satisfactorily or sufficiently to the *money* motivation described above. Try the next inducement on him: his potential or actual interest in job security.

My experience coincides with that of the majority of management specialists regarding the impact of this motivation on most employees. I place it as second only to *money*.

The authorities generally agree that most employees are interested in the assurance that they won't lose their jobs. This is true in the face of the seemingly large number of people who *voluntarily* change jobs.

Analyze This Motivation Carefully

You can make profitable motivational use of an employee's desire to continue to work in the company where he now finds himself. Distinguish carefully between the inducement I am *now* discussing and the one I've just finished dealing with above, regarding *money*.

Seize the Opportunity

Here is how you can take advantage of a man's interest in *job security,* to get him to do better and/or more. This is wholly aside from the question of whether he can earn more money. And it goes above and beyond the situation where if he fails to meet acceptable standards, he may be downgraded or separated.

Let Him Know the Facts

Here are suggestions for capitaliztng on a man's natural desire to stay on in the same company:

- Point out to every employee that as long as he satisfies specified performance standards he can continue to work in this company for the rest of his active business life. Tell him so just before hiring him and/or whenever you feel he needs this additional motivation.
- Emphasize that this company—and you—judge and treat the employee solely on the basis of results and attitudes. No one loses his job, or an opportunity to progress, for any personal or categorical reason. The only strike against him can be consistent failure to meet established standards.
- Stress the peace of mind that this can give him, both on the job and away from it.
- If applicable, explain to him that your company's position in the economic world is solid. There is very little likelihood that he'd have to be downgraded or separated because of loss of business.

- Then convince him that:
  - —He owes it to himself and the company constantly to do his best, in return for the security on the job that it gives him.
  - —Only through such an attitude and such results can the company continue to prosper.

Be Negative If You Have to

If an employee continues to fail to yield desired results, and he doesn't respond to the *job-security* motivation (*or* the *money* motivation), you'd better:

1. Point out to him your dissatisfaction with his performance.
2. Warn him that he must improve or suffer the consequences.
3. Apply the necessary discipline if he persists in failing to yield the indicated results.

HARNESS SATISFACTIONS TO MOTIVATION

You mustn't give up if *money* and *job security* don't motivate your men sufficiently. Before you follow the suggestions above, regarding people who just *won't* respond to those two inducements, have a go at the factors I'm now about to discuss. Also, if *money* and/or *job security* yield only *partial* results, use *satisfactions* as a supplementary motivating force.

My experience has shown that this is usually necessary.

Recognize Motivation Priorities

My reason for treating this kind of motivation in third place is that most of the employees I've come across consider it only after they've thought about *money* and *job security*.

Before outlining the points of the "satisfactions" motivation, here are two diametrically-different, relevant cases which I've come across in my consulting work:

CASE NUMBER ONE involves Leonard Boyd, who told me:

"Why should I knock myself out for my boss? He doesn't care about me. He never gives me credit for a good job well done. But he sure lets me know real quickly and loudly when I've goofed. And if he signs his name to one of my reports, he's the only one that gets top-brass praise."

CASE NUMBER TWO concerns Howard Larson.

Why does Howard always "work his fingers to the bone"?

He likes and respects his boss. He knows that his own performance and results reflect on his boss's ability to account favorably to *his* superior. Therefore, Howard realizes that how *he* takes care of his *own* bailiwick will help determine how another man, about whose success he cares, will look in the eyes of that *other* man's boss.

So, following the basic principles of logic, Howard feels and acts this way:

- I want *my* boss to look good in *his* boss's eyes.
- I can help control this, in part, by what *my* boss can report about *my* results.
- So I'm jolly well going to do my best for that reason, if for no other.

Put "Satisfactions" to Work

Regardless of *why* you want to use *satisfactions* (I call them *psychic* satisfactions) for motivation, here's how they work:

- Consistently practice the right kind of relationships with your subordinates. They will generally respond with the right kind of productivity.
- If a man begins to demonstrate, by his performance, that he doesn't really *want* to do his best/most, point out to him:
  —Any appropriate *money/job-security* motivations which may be applicable; *and*
  —That you want to continue to treat him right and can do so only if he holds up his end of the mutual relationship.

Handle Your Men Wisely

Now to enlarge on the first point made above.

If you treat your men right they'll generally treat *you* right and give you the consistent productivity you want.

Here's what you must do to achieve this goal:

STEP NUMBER ONE

In your every-day relationships with them, act toward them—and treat them—in such a way that they respect (and, preferably, also like) you.

On page 199 is a checklist on behavior (toward subordinates) of the kind which will establish and maintain the sort of relationship I'm referring to. As you go down the list in the left-hand column, rate yourself on how closely you come to fulfilling the requirements called for. Fill in the columns to the right.

How I can establish and maintain desirable every-day relationships with my subordinates:	I am now doing entirely satisfactorily with all of my people:	I can do more or better, in this connection, with some or all of my people, as follows:
a. Be firm, fair and consistent.		
b. Treat my men with respect and dignity.		
c. Be and show myself interested in their progress and well-being.		
d. Be calm and patient.		
e. Speak to them courteously and with even temper.		
f. Praise them whenever they deserve it—publicly, if this is desirable.		
g. Criticize or correct them (constructively) only when appropriate—and privately.		
h. Be friendly with all of them, but don't be a personal friend of any of them.		
i. Don't be too familiar with them.		
j. Act in a dignified manner at all times.		
k. Listen to them whenever they want to talk, although not to excess.		
l. Be effective in communications with them.		
m. Back them up whenever possible.		
n. Don't bypass them by issuing orders, instructions or criticisms to *their* subordinates.		
o. Whenever possible, grant their reasonable requests.		
p. Defend them before my superior whenever this is called for and justified.		
q. Be reasonable in giving them assignments.		

STEP NUMBER TWO

Let them know that *their* performance and results may affect your own success on the job. If you treat them as suggested above, they'll *care* about how you look in the eyes of your superior. Any time they do less or worse than they're capable of, all you have to do is tell them that they're letting you down. You can then indicate that they can help you, rather than hinder you, by doing more or better.

STEP NUMBER THREE

In order to make sure that they *consistently* want to reach and utilize their maximum/optimum capacities, point out to them the great satisfactions they can derive from knowing that they're always doing their most and best.

Eight Key Satisfactions that you can refer to are:

1. The knowledge that they are always doing the most and the best they can for the good of the company. This makes them feel good because they're fulfilling themselves completely, are being kept at a high pitch of interest and excitement, and are doing the right and honorable thing in return for their salaries and other company benefits.

2. The pride they take in good workmanship, in achievement and in solving difficult problems.

3. The challenge to their ingenuity, creativity, energy, exertions and abilities. And the joy of meeting that challenge.

4. The pleasure they derive from knowing that their boss, and the latter's superiors, know how conscientious and successful the lower-level men are.

5. The satisfaction of knowing that their colleagues realize that they more than carry their weight. And that they are making a major contribution to the joint efforts of all.

6. The respect they get from their subordinates, because the latter know of their boss's right-minded attitudes and activities.

7. The respect and admiration of their family, friends and acquaintances. They can hold their heads high among them, because they know that they're always striving for the best possible results.

8. The pleasure they get from knowing that they're making an ever-more-valuable contribution to the well-being of their country and their community.

It Can Work

Here's a case I witnessed which effectively illustrates the general idea.

Strike!

The month was October. The place was a large factory. The occasion was an unexpected "wildcat" strike.

A union member on the midnight shift had been dismissed for refusal to obey his foreman's lawful order. At 5 A.M. the Chief Shop Steward told the Shift Foreman that he was advising the union members not to do any work on *any* shift until the discharged worker was fully reinstated, without loss of pay.

At 7 A.M. the regular shift began coming into the plant. Time cards were located in each department.

WISE TREATMENT BEGINS

I happened to be talking with the Day Foreman of one of those departments, from 6:45 A.M. on. As his men came toward him, one at a time, he told *each one of them* substantially the following:

"Morning, Joe" (or Pete, etc.) "Your Union has called an informal work stoppage. Sorry they didn't have a chance to let you know sooner. If you like, you can put your things in your locker, but please don't punch in. You can go to the coffee shop and relax until your Union officials get word to you."

The "strike" was settled that afternoon.

EVERYONE KNEW

Starting the next day, I held my usual seminars with the lower management men I was working with. There were 75 of these in all, so we had five different groups.

Each day when I met with another group, I talked about the incident with that foreman as an example of good human relations. I said nothing which would give any clue as to whom I was talking about.

A few days later I met my foreman friend again. He said:

"Hey, Bill. At least fifteen men from your seminars have told me you were talking about me this week."

OFFER PROMOTIONS REALISTICALLY

You will, of course, want to make use of every effective inducement at your disposal. In addition to *money, job security* and *psychic satisfactions,* you may find it advisable to use *an opportunity to be promoted* as a motivation.

Use Your Judgment

For those people to whom this is applicable, the relationship between satisfactory results and opportunities for a higher position can be pointed out. Emphasize the greater challenge and prestige of the *position,* rather than any greater amount of money that might be involved.

The theme would then be: Among the reasons why you should want to work harder and better is that you might then qualify for one of the many (or several) opportunities for promotion which keep on coming up in this company.

Limit Your Encouragement

But before you use such opportunities as motivation, you must consider the limitations on the effectiveness of that inducement.

One such restriction can be humorously illustrated by the old gag about the immigrant who joined the local political club. He was very active and got a tremendous number of votes for the party. One day he came to the Club Leader and said: "Please make me a Councilman."

AMBITION ASSERTS ITSELF

Nomination to candidacy from that party, in that district, was tantamount to election, so our friend became a Councilman. When he'd finished his term, he said: "I want you to do me another favor. Make me a Congressman."

Toward the end of his term he said to the Leader: "And now another favor, please. Make me a U.S. Senator."

THE PEAK ACHIEVED

Toward the end of his term as Senator, he came to his leader once more. Here was the conversation between them:

> *The Senator:*   "I want you to do me another favor."
> *The Leader:*   "Sorry. I can't make you President!"
> *The Senator:*   "I don't want you to make me President. All I want you
>   to do is make me a citizen."

Know Whom to Induce

You're getting ready to try to motivate some of your people by talking to them about possible promotion as a reward for maximum/optimum results. Before doing so, review the following facts, subscribed to by all successful management specialists:

- Not everyone wants to aspire to, or work harder in, a higher position.
- A Manager shouldn't offer an opportunity for promotion to a subordinate unless he's reasonably sure he can keep his promise.
- You may not *want* certain of your men promoted.

Use "Promotion" Properly

Here's how you can successfully use *opportunity for promotion* as motivation:

1. As far as possible, make effective use of the other inducements I've already talked about: *money, job security* and *psychic satisfactions.*
2. Analyze your situation and make sure that:
   a. There *are* positions available into which some of your subordinates can be promoted within a reasonable period of time.
   b. The men to whom you would offer promotion opportunities, as an inducement, are the kind you'd like to see in such higher positions.

    c. Such men are, or can be influenced to become, ambitious for such promotion.

3. Point out to qualified subordinates that continued maximum/optimum exertion and desirable results *can* lead to their promotion.

Tell them that you'll watch them very carefully for this purpose, and reward those who merit it. But ask them to remember that you're not in a position to *promise* them anything. *And* that whether they get the promotion or not, they'll always want to do their best and most anyway, since they're the kind of people they are.

MOTIVATE BEFORE PROMOTING

If you decide that you want to and can offer a promotion to a particular subordinate, you must take still another step before you reward him for his past performance. The reason for this is that you want to make sure that he continues to yield, in the new job, the kind of results which he produced on the current one.

Prepare for the Offer

Here are the steps you should take before actually naming a man to a higher post:

FIRST STEP

Call him in to have a talk with you before you and he agree about his appointment to the higher job.

SECOND STEP

Without oratory, but in clear terms, make a "speech" to him somewhat along these lines:

"Joe, I'm seriously considering having you appointed.... As you know, this would represent an advancement for you.

"But before I give you the job, and before you decide to take it, we ought to come to a complete understanding of what's involved, and of what I'd expect of you, in the new post."

Bring in the RAA

"If you become . . . you'll be required to undertake satisfactorily the following responsibilities, authority and accountability: . . . .

"I think you're the man for the position, and I have every confidence you'll be able to do a real bang-up job in it. I, for my part, will always make it perfectly clear to you what I expect of you. I'll see to it that you always know how to do well whatever I ask you to do. And you'll always have all the facilities you need for the work."

Emphasize His Role

"Now, Joe, you and I both know that you're a very capable man. This is an important job, and it makes an important contribution to my own ability to perform as my superior expects *me* to, and as I want to perform.

"In this position I need and can afford to have, only a man who is always prepared to exert himself to his fullest and best capacities. He will always do his best and his most. And, of course, this must be along the lines I lay down for him."

Point Out the Advantages

"Joe, the man who does this for me will be very happy in his work. He will...." (Here review with him the other three motivations I've talked about above.)

"Now, Joe, if you take this job, it must be with a complete understanding of what I've just said and complete agreement with what I want.

"Joe, do you want the job under those conditions?"

THIRD STEP

Answer any questions Joe may have. But don't give him the higher job unless you're reasonably sure he *can* and *will* do what you ask.

FOURTH STEP

Then you can congratulate him, assure him of your confidence in him and tell him how happy you are to have him aboard.

TACKLE THE LAGGARD

Next, here's a technique for dealing with a subordinate who's beginning to show that he's being less well-motivated than you want him to be.

Pay Special Attention to the "Old-Timer"

A sound approach to this is illustrated by what I saw Clayt Killoran do.

Here's how he handled the "Old-Timer" who was beginning to lose interest in his job.

FIRST, INVESTIGATE

Clayt would find out why the man was slipping, and try to eliminate as many causes as he could.

But when he was convinced that the slowdown was due only to poor attitudes, he'd read him the riot act. He'd point out that the man couldn't afford in his later years to besmirch his previously good record. And he always managed to find a way of letting him know that the years of satisfactory performance up to that time didn't compensate for present and future losses to company profitability.

THEN BE POSITIVE

Clayt would end on a note of optimism and try to inspire the man to go back to the "good old" ways.

SPEAK TO THEM ALL

Here's how to handle a man who has never heard the kind of "speech" referred to above, and who has been showing a consistent lessening of desire to do his best and most.

Call him into the office and make *this* kind of "speech" to him:

"Pete, I'm sorry to have to tell you that during the last few months you've shown no change in the attitude I've discussed with you on several occasions."

Remind Him of Your Previous Chats

"As I told you then, so I'm telling you now. You *must* justify your salary and other company privileges. I can't continue to approve spending company money on you and your activities unless you consistently give me the most and the best of which you're capable.

"Now, I'm prepared to help you in any way I can, and I'm confident that you can meet the requirements I've set for you."

Explain the Alternatives

"But I want you to know that if you continue to have the attitude I've so frequently called to your attention, I'll have to recommend that you be put into a job where what you want to do is enough for the salary and other benefits that *that* job offers.

"Now, Pete, let's forget that I ever had to talk to you this way. I know that it won't be necessary for me to bring this matter up again."

FOLLOW UP ON MOTIVATION

After making one or another of those "speeches," you'll want to observe, and act on, how *they* react to the talks.

- If the new man works out right, or the older man "shapes up and flies right," you've accomplished your mission and one word was worth a thousand pictures.
- On the other hand, if your "speeches" *don't* yield the results you wanted, you have a perfect setup for the next step in your motivational campaign.

For the Newer Subordinate

Let's take, first, the new man. Just as soon as it becomes obvious that he's not responding satisfactorily to *any* of the motivations you've applied to him, call him in.

Tell him you've analyzed his attitudes. Then remind him of the "speech" you made to him. Ask him whether he intends to change his attitude and his performance to the way you want. If his answer is *yes,* encourage him and express confidence in his ability to make the grade.

For the "Older" Subordinate

Next, take the "older" man. If he begins to show either a continuation of, or a reversion to, the undesirable attitudes which prompted you to make the "speech" that you did, remind him of it. Then proceed as described in the preceding paragraph.

For Both of Them

Finally, if either the newer man *or* the "older" man *still* fails to meet your standards, you have a perfectly valid reason for applying disciplinary action. No one will be able to accuse you of not having given him fair warning.

MOTIVATE IN DEPTH

As you do with every other management responsibility, so, too, will you want to practice the in-depth penetration of motivation.

I've talked, here, about how *you* might effectively motivate your *immediate* subordinates. In addition to doing that, you *must* see to it that *they* properly motivate *their* immediate subordinates. And even *that* isn't enough.

Go All the Way

You must also see to it that your *immediate subordinates* see to it that *their* immediate subordinates engage in proper motivation below them. Your responsibility for in-depth motivation ends only when, as a result of *your* efforts, each of your successive subordinate levels properly motivates each of *his* successive subordinate levels. And this must go all the way down until, finally, *non-management* is properly motivated.

Communication Is the Factor

To accomplish this you must let your immediate subordinates know that they must see to it that this message is properly communicated and followed through, all the way down their respective lines.

Then, as you supervise on all levels below you, keep on the lookout against inadequate motivation on any level. If you see it, you can point this out to your immediate subordinates, for remedial action by them. And you can check up later to see whether there has been any improvement.

SUCCESS CAPSULE NUMBER FOURTEEN

In this *Success Factor* I've discussed *how* you can effectively meet your responsibilities for *motivating* your subordinates.

1. You must see to it that your subordinates constantly exert themselves to their fullest and best capacities along lines you set down, and effectively communicated to them.
2. Before you do or say anything to motivate them for this purpose, you must set the stage properly by:
    a. Making perfectly clear to them what you expect of them.
    b. Effectively explaining to them exactly how to accomplish this satisfactorily.
    c. Seeing to it that they have all the facilities they need in order to do the job well.
3. Check to be sure that you know which of your men are Self-Motivators and which are not.
4. Bear in mind that the four basic motivations which you can apply to your men are: money, job security, psychic satisfactions, promotion.
5. Use each of those motivations wisely:
    a. Offer more money for better results where you can. Where you can't, equate the man's remuneration to his consistent production of at least minimum acceptable standards of performance. Make it clear that his persistent failure can result in transfer, demotion or separation.

b. Point out to your men that as long as they perform satisfactorily they have a secure job in the company, free from individual discrimination of any kind. In return for this assurance they should exert themselves to their fullest and best capacities. Besides, the better their results, the greater their chances of contributing to the company's stability and their own job security.

c. Treat your people in such a way that they will *care* about the success of *your* department. They will then *want* to do well so that, among other reasons, *you* will look good in your boss's eyes. Then, too, appeal to their basic interest in gleaning psychic satisfactions from their work, so that they'll want to work better in order to feel those satisfactions.

d. Offer an opportunity for promotion as an inducement for better results, only to those people who:

1) Are qualified for higher positions which can become vacant (or be created); and

2) Are genuinely interested in such an opportunity.

6. Follow up on your motivation and remind laggards of the reasons why they should do better. Follow up, too, on your reminders, so you can evaluate and act on the results.

7. Make sure that the motivation you initiate with your immediate subordinates ultimately reaches all the way down, through channels, to your line non-management people.

How You Can
Supervise Successfully

This *Success Factor* takes up the techniques you can employ to make sure that your men are doing what you want them to.

Since your objective is to get consistently-high profitable productivity from your subordinates, always see to it that they:

- Know exactly what's expected of them.
- Know how to do this well.
- Have all the facilities they need for this.
- Really *want* to do the best and the most of which they are capable.

GO ONE STEP FURTHER

It's one thing to follow all the steps necessary to bring those four results about. But it's another to know whether what you want your men to do actually gets done the way you wanted it.

You might ask me: "But aren't you going too far? After all, if my men know and understand all that they have to do; if they have what they need in order to do it; and if they want to do it well; what more can I ask?"

Avoid Unwise Assumptions

It's surprising how many times there is *much* more you can ask. Whatever you may do or say, many things can happen between the time you finish your planning, communication, training and motivation activities for a particular assignment, and the time that your subordinates are in a position to finish that assignment satisfactorily.

Follow Through

Another way of saying the same thing is this: When you've said and done all you can to get the men started on the job, you've no way of being really sure whether they're making the kind of progress you want, unless you periodically check up on them. Many things can happen to prevent them from doing the work right. And they won't always come to you to tell you that the job isn't progressing on schedule.

If you wait until the deadline you've established for the finished job before finding out how it's proceeding, you may discover at that time that your men are way behind schedule. And you'll probably realize that you could have prevented this delay if you'd intervened earlier.

Does this mean that your subordinates aren't *capable* of doing what they were supposed to? Not necessarily. But it does mean that they may be unable to do a *particular job* properly without letting you know that fact as early as you would have liked them to.

Look Before It's Too Late

Two cases, one negative and one positive, show how important it is to check up promptly.

The Wrong Way

Eric Williams, Operations Manager of a multi-product manufacturing company, told me one day how he'd learned his lesson to check up on assignments.

The Sales Department had finally landed a contract with a company it had been after for several years. The new customer had indicated that this was to be a trial order. If the manufacturer could give them the units they wanted, strictly according to specs, and within the designated time, there would probably be much more business, profitable business.

THE FIRST STEPS

Eric called in the superintendent in charge of that particular fabricating department and explained to him in great detail not only what was to be done, but also how important this was to the company. The superintendent was an old hand at the game, and had a fine record of coming through on all requests.

Eric knew how reliable that man was and therefore felt that he could just leave the order in his hands and wait until it was finished. He had other things to do, with less-reliable subordinates.

A Surprise Development

The next thing that hit Eric was a wild howl from the Sales Manager. The finished units had *not* met specifications, although they had come close, and the customer had sworn they would never do business with them again.

On checking up, Eric found that a problem had come up which could have been resolved by finishing the job a bit later than specified. The superintendent, being proud of his ability to make his own decisions, had taken it upon himself to authorize a slight departure from the specs, one which he honestly believed would be satisfactory to the customer.

The Result

Well, it wasn't. And who got the blame? Eric. And *was* it his fault? Yes. He knows this now. He should have required certain periodic reports, and should have made interim inquiries, especially when the situation involved a new customer on a trial basis.

The Right Way

Now I'll tell you what happened in Hank Oliphant's company.

A customer was complaining that the units he'd ordered were beginning to be delivered too late for his needs. And Cost Control was complaining that the department manufacturing those units was beginning to overrun its budget.

Hank immediately added to existing controls a simple reporting system.

Flow of Information

At the beginning of every business day two reports had to be on his desk; if they weren't, he'd go after his subordinates to get them.

One report showed whether the production scheduled for the day before was right on time. And if not, why not and what was being done about it.

The other report showed how many dollars had been spent against budget the day before. And if there was an overrun, how much, why, and how this would be made up for on another day.

PLAN YOUR SUPERVISION

The first principle of supervision I'd like to present is this:

Just as soon as you have assigned a task to one of your subordinates—with all the effective communication, training and motivation needed for the job—immediately plan a program for checking up on how he is progressing. You can't, of course, spend *all* your time following up on him, but you can't afford to spend *too little* time on it either.

You can't devote too much time to any one subordinate, but you can't *neglect* any one subordinate.

Get Out Among Your Men

"I'm tied down to my office practically all day. I don't have the time to go out and visit my subordinates."

"My boss is always sending for me and keeping me in his office. I can't even get my paper work done."

"I'm always attending meetings. How do you expect me to check up on my men?"

Famous last words!

Master Your Supervisory Time

You can pretty much decide for yourself what to do and when to do it. And if you complain you're short on time you might count up the minutes and hours you spend on things far less important than supervising your line.

Two Cardinal Principles

1. You *must* have time to check up on how your subordinates are making out.
2. You *can* find time for this through proper planning and proportionate allocation of your attention among the various things you have to do.

Make the Time

The key to having enough time for supervising subordinates is to attend to all your *other* responsibilities only when it isn't important to be supervising. My experience has convinced me that if you had to select *one* responsibility as your greatest, it would be *supervision*.

Overcome Time Obstacles

Of course you *must* have time to be with your boss when he wants you. And you *have to* consult with your colleagues. You *need* to make plans for delegating tasks to your men. You *want* to explain to them *what* they are to do and *how* to do it. You *can't* avoid your obligation to motivate them.

But, if you add up all of those activities you should still have time to do all the supervising necessary for assuring success.

Weigh Your Requirements

Part of the secret is how you allocate your time among your various subordinates. You must pay attention to all, but some require more and some less.

A TECHNIQUE

To help you get into the habit of taking care of *all* of your other responsibilities, and still undertake and properly fulfill your most important obligation—supervising your subordinates—a suggested "Time-Planner" is presented on page 214. You can, if you like, use it—or some modification of it—on a day-to-day or week-to-week basis. It can help you find or make time to do everything you want to, in the proper proportions.

Some Relevant Cases

When the subject of supervision arose, I learned to talk to Val Emmons about it.

Val didn't believe that management men had to be checked up on. It wasn't dignified. Besides, it wasn't necessary.

Did Val know what was going on all the time? No.

How did he get away with it? He didn't.

THE INEVITABLE RESULT

Val is still a member of his company's Management Team, but he's no longer responsible for *human* productivity.

He spends most of his time in the office he likes so much, shuffling papers. They're important papers, all right, which is why a *management* man must be responsible for them.

But Val doesn't have to change his mind about supervising management men. None of them reports to him.

A Different Approach

Every now and then I meet a manager like Ermon Rankin. Erm was completely sold on the importance of always knowing what was going on among his subordinates.

If you asked him at any one time who was doing what, or how a par-

Date	*From (time)*	*To (time)*	*I must be with (person's name)*	*I should be physically supervising (subordinate's name)*	*I should be analyzing reports from (subordinate's name)*	*I can spend on*		
						Planning new assignments for (names)	*Communicating new assignments (to names)*	*Other activities (specify)*

ticular project was coming along, he always had the answer for you—accurate and complete.

How He Did It

How come? Erm made it his business to know. You mightn't have been able to see him much in his office, although his secretary always knew where he was. But you may be sure that Erm was somewhere in the middle of the action.

Result? Nothing went wrong for very long before Erm knew about it and was in there pitching to get it back on the right track.

CHECK UP CORRECTLY

There's no such thing as *one* exclusive way of finding out what's going on. Business requires *several* different techniques, each fitted to specific requirements.

One of the qualities of a good Manager is that he knows *all* the ways to check up on his men and always uses the one best suited to a particular situation.

Four Practicable Ways

I know of at least four easy methods for checking up on subordinates:

1. Being physically present among them frequently and long enough to know exactly what's going on.
2. Requiring specific kinds of reports from them and studying these very carefully.
3. Asking them to come in and talk to you, from time to time, individually and in meetings.
4. Using the phone or a memo.

Which Path Is Best?

Now comes the question: When should you use the one method rather than another?

A helpful rule of thumb might be:

- Be among your men as often as possible.
- Require only those reports which are meaningful, and study each one carefully.
- On the few occasions when you have to be in your office, ask specific men to come in and talk to you about the progress of their work and/or about their problems.

- Call meetings only when they can make an important contribution to your department, and then *only* at times when they don't interfere with productivity. Make the meetings short. And use meetings for *finding out* as well as for telling.

An Illustration

When I worked for a company which conducted seminars for other companies' Managers, I had a group of salesmen who were supposed to sell my services as a seminar leader.

On one occasion we were offering a special seminar on how to run effective meetings. Our salesmen were sent out to call on Top Management men in prospective companies, and try to sell them on sending one or more of their subordinates to this seminar.

Why He Wasn't Around

One of my salesmen told me that when he'd explained his message in one company, a vice president said: "I have just the man. He's going to have to conduct a great many meetings for us. I'd like you to talk to him. Wait a moment and I'll try to get him up here."

Our salesman never succeeded in enlisting that man in a seminar on how to run meetings. He was always attending meetings.

MAXIMIZE YOUR SUPERVISORY TIME

My experience has convinced me that the Manager most likely to succeed is the one who spends a *minimum* of time in his office. *Some* time he *must* spend there, of course. And I don't have to tell anyone *when* he should be there. My goal is to persuade you to be *away* from your office as much as possible, so you can be *physically present* among your people *most* of the time.

Three Suggestions for Success

1. Plan and organize your time and work in such a way that you need to spend very little time in your office.
2. Whenever you're about to leave your office, let your secretary know where you'll be.
3. Get out and circulate among your subordinates. Spend as much time with them as you can.

A Question

When I gave this advice to a particular management man, he asked: "How do I keep myself busy and productive while I'm with my men?" Here's how I answered him.

There are at least a dozen activities a Manager can engage in while dividing his time and attention among his immediate subordinates—in *their* departments, and not in his own office. If you want to be profitably productive while physically with your men:

1. Look around at what's going on and come to specific conclusions about the progress and/or problems observed.
2. Listen to a subordinate and absorb what he says.
3. See whether there's any activity which *should* be taking place but isn't, and find out why.
4. Get to the bottom of the *reasons* for anything that isn't coming along exactly as it should.
5. Come to a conclusion on what needs to be done about any problems noticed or called to your attention.
6. Find out what people are saying, thinking and/or feeling, and why.
7. Come to a conclusion about who, if anybody, needs special or more frequent observation or watching.
8. Decide *who* should be praised and/or rewarded for exceptionally good work.
9. Make up your mind about *who* is to be corrected, helped, guided or further directed, and in what way.
10. Come to a conclusion about *who* should be criticized, warned and/or disciplined.
11. Add to your store of impressions on *who* looks promising for promotion or advancement.
12. Do everything possible to keep morale on a high level.

EVALUATE YOUR SUPERVISORY HABITS

You may find the procedure given on page 218 helpful: For the next few weeks, keep a record of your visits to your immediate subordinates. As soon as possible after you leave any one of them, fill in the appropriate blanks on the form below.

Then, after the two weeks are up, compare the activities you recorded with the twelve preceding suggestions.

| Date | Time | | Person visited | What I did while I was with him |
	From	To		

PUT TACT INTO YOUR CONTACT

It's always interesting to me to compare different Managers' techniques for checking up on their men.

One Type

Take Rupert Petty. The only time that Rupert went to see an immediate subordinate was when something had gone wrong. On such occasions Rupert would storm into a department, stride right over to its head and barge right in with his complaint, at the top of his voice.

Another Type

On the other hand, there's Gene Cummings. You could never tell, if you saw him walking around in the areas for which he was responsible, what he had on his mind. You hardly ever stopped to think about it. Gene just seemed to belong there. He accomplished what he intended to, but no apple carts were upset.

What You Must Do

- You've *got* to spend a great deal of time among your people.
- Your presence there mustn't unnerve anyone.
- You must, while with them, exercise *full* supervisory functions.

How You Can Do It

1. Be around your subordinates so frequently that no one is surprised to see you there. They should take it for granted that you belong there. Your presence shouldn't cause anyone to wonder what you're doing there.

2. From the moment that you approach an area where one of your subordinates functions, until you're out of sight (on your way back from there), act naturally. Walk calmly and slowly. Have a neutral expression on your face. Make it seem that you're there only because—well, where else should you be?

3. Never show by expression, bearing, manner or word what you're thinking, as you go around observing and listening to everyone and everything.

4. Be casual in your conversations, keep your voice even and don't show any emotion if you suddenly see something out of the ordinary.

5. Ask questions as though you're merely seeking to be informed about what's perfectly natural.

6. Interpolate questions and statements of a friendly nature among your more pointed inquiries.

7. If you want to be forceful about something that you've seen or heard, arrange to draw your subordinate aside unnoticeably, and talk to him about it in such a way that no one else is aware of what you're doing.

SUPERVISE IN DEPTH

Up to now, when I talked about management in depth, I pointed out only one responsibility: to see to it that your communications and motivations were properly carried on all the way down your line. But when I mention *supervision* in depth, I have to add another dimension.

A Case in Point

I must say a word about Craig Stevens. He was General Manager of a large airplane-overhaul base.

Craig was conscientious, loyal and hard-working. But he didn't like to leave his office. Inside he was always busy with the activities he most enjoyed. Outside—well, if he went out he might run into problems which he preferred to have his *subordinates* solve. Two situations in which I was personally involved point up the shortcomings that Craig had because of his attitude toward in-depth supervision.

THE FIRST WEAKNESS

To begin with, everywhere I went in the company, men would tell me something like this:

"We don't even know what Mr. Stevens looks like. No doubt he's a fine man, but he's apparently not interested in us.

"Did you know Mr. Brack, his predecessor? *There* was a Manager for you! Every day he'd walk through the hangars and the yard saying *hello* to everybody. We worked real hard for him, because we knew that he was interested in us."

THE SECOND WEAKNESS

The other situation dramatically demonstrates why a Manager must be constantly moving about on all levels below him.

One day I had to go from one hangar to another. There were catwalks connecting them, so that you didn't have to go down the stairs from one hangar to go up the stairs in the next one.

While I was crossing one of these catwalks—about four stories high— I happened to glance down. This was the scene I witnessed.

THE UNOBSERVED FOREMEN

In the passageway between the two hangars two foremen were standing and talking to each other. It didn't look like a business conversation. Each one had his back to his own hangar.

On the fuselage of one of the planes in the hangar I could see two mechanics talking to each other, facing the two foremen. That didn't look like a business conversation either.

THE OBSERVANT MECHANICS

The moment that the two foremen began to separate to return to their respective posts, the two mechanics separated. When their boss came by he couldn't have guessed that they'd just recently been goofing off.

When the cat's away. . . .

UNDERTAKE TOTAL SUPERVISION

Now for the two facets of supervision in depth mentioned above.

1. *You* must see to it that your *immediate subordinates* see to it that *their* immediate subordinates see to it—and so on, down through front-line management—that every higher management man in your line is properly supervising his immediate subordinates. *You* can accomplish this by impressing on your immediate subordinates that each of them must see to it that the message is effectively carried on all the way down the line.

2. To describe the *second* facet of in-depth supervision I'll begin with the organization chart on page 222.

(You'll have no difficulty fitting your own situation into it. In analyzing and following this chart, simply eliminate any level or levels not applicable to your own case. If your situation requires one or more *additional* lower levels of management, simply supply them on the chart.)

Eight Depth Steps

1. So plan and organize your time and commitments so that you can visit every level below you with maximum possible periodicity and frequency.

2. Tell each of your Level No. 2 men that you plan periodically to be moving about among *their* subordinates, all the way down the line. Point out that you intend to do this only because you want to keep your hand in and maintain the kind of personal touch which will strengthen *their own* effectiveness. Assure them that you won't issue any instructions or orders, tell anyone how to do anything, or express any judgments to

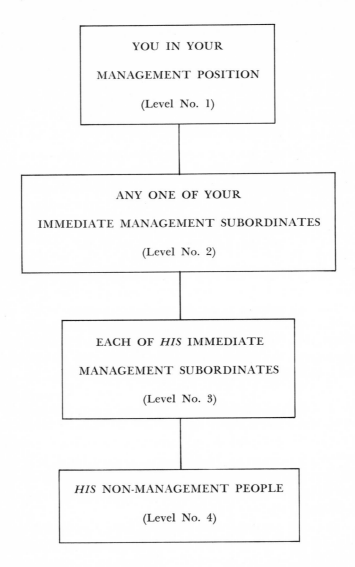

anyone visited. Promise them, also, that you'll always report to them on your findings.

3. If convenient, let your No. 2 men know the dates and times that you plan to make those visits. But if you have reason to suspect that a surprise visit is better, simply don't inform them in advance.

4. When you approach any Level No. 3 man, greet him and make sure he knows that your visit is with the knowledge and approval of his

Level No. 2 superior. Ask him how things are coming along, find out for yourself the status of progress and problems, and do everything possible to boost his morale. Whatever you do or say, act in complete consistency with his superior's way of managing him. Don't issue any instructions except in cases of emergency. If No. 2 is temporarily absent, and you *must* issue instructions, tell No. 3 that you're acting *for* No. 2 and will inform the latter about it when he gets back.

   5. Tell No. 3 that you intend to visit with No. 4. Make the same kind of explanation to him about your proposed visits, that you did to No. 2 about No. 3. And act with No. 4 exactly as you did with No. 3.

   6. Report to No. 2 on both the positive and negative aspects of your observations on Levels 3 and 4. Let 2 make all corrections and take all necessary steps to improve functioning on those lower levels.

   7. Follow up on No. 2 to make sure that significant recommendations made by you to him have been properly carried out.

   8. Start the process all over again and keep it up all the time.

SUCCESS CAPSULE NUMBER FIFTEEN

In this *Success Factor* I emphasized the following points:

1. You must *continually and periodically* check up on the progress and problems of your immediate subordinates. You shouldn't wait to do this only on or after any deadlines you may have established for the tasks assigned.

2. You must so plan and organize your time and activities that you *can* effectively supervise your subordinates with the necessary frequency.

3. You can find out what's going on below you in a number of ways:
    a. Physical presence among your men.
    b. Reports from them to you.
    c. Individual conferences in your office at your request.
    d. Meetings during which you devote sufficient time to followup.
    e. The phone, or memos, when these are the best channels for finding out what's going on.

4. You should select those methods of supervision which are most effective at particular times and in particular circumstances.

5. But nothing can take the place of frequent *physical* presence among your subordinates.

6. While physically present among them you should:
    a. Find out what's going on, and why.

    b. Come to specific decisions or conclusions on what followup, if any, you want to make as a result of what you've observed or discovered.

    c. Constantly evaluate your subordinates.

    d. Keep morale as high as possible.

7. When you're physically present among your men, as a supervisor, you must be natural and subtle about your actions and statements. You must find out what's going on without upsetting anyone.

8. You must make sure that your immediate subordinates see to it that proper supervision is exercised by each appropriate management man, all the way down the line. But you yourself must also supervise every level, from the one just below you all the way down through non-management. When you do so, however, you must strictly observe and follow the rules for respecting levels of authority and responsibility.

How You Can Profitably Follow Up on Supervision

This *Success Factor* discusses the steps you must take in order to capitalize on your observations and reactions during supervision.

A Case in Point

Norbert Ellis was the most dedicated supervisor I'd ever met. He was *always* with his subordinates. He knew *everything* that was going on. The only trouble was that he was so busy accumulating information that he seldom got around to making valuable use of it.

Another Case

Brian Powers, on the other hand, planned his visits to his men in such a way that he had time and energy to do what his observations called for. He kept good records of his supervisory findings; but he also *acted* quite promptly where action was indicated.

DO SOMETHING ABOUT WHAT YOU FIND OUT

The trouble with many Managers is *not* that they don't *know* enough about what's going on below, but that they don't *do* enough about it—the right things done at the right time. This common failure often comes from inertia, if not from an unwillingness to face facts and possible unpleasantness.

225

Any boss, no matter how kind-hearted he may be, *must* take seriously the results of his supervision, and translate them into action where this is called for.

Six Followup Steps

Here's what you must do after any *one* supervisory stint:

1. Analyze what's been learned.
2. Decide what to do about it (in addition to the interim decisions reached while supervising).
3. Do what has to be done: promptly, wisely and thoroughly.
4. Check up on whether what's been done has been effective. And if it hasn't been, do whatever is needed to *make* it effective.
5. Supervise once more to see whether the steps taken have led to the desired results.
6. Continue the process in a "beneficent circle."

What to Do While Still Supervising

Some of the things that can be done to follow up on what's been learned through face-to-face supervision, are best undertaken while the supervisor is still physically present among the subordinates about whom he has made his findings. This kind of followup can include:

- Praising people who deserve to be commended for exceptional performance.
- Telling the men that they're on the right track, and should continue that way.
- Pointing out to one or more immediate subordinates—privately and tactfully—that they are not going about a particular task in the best way, and that they should do it as it is now going to be explained to them.
- Telling the men that they will soon get the additional or different facilities they need.
- Providing any additional or different motivation feasible at that moment.
- Pointing out—again, privately and tactfully—ways of improving their performance regarding safety, housekeeping, quality, time for completion of the task, cost reduction and/or morale.
- Telling them that you will be back again soon to see how they've improved as a result of your suggestions.
- Making arrangements for them to come and see you for specific, helpful or corrective suggestions.

An Example of Inadequacy

An executive I knew had a Supervisory Engineer in his line whose product knowledge and technological skill were vital to his manufacturing responsibility. *And* he was difficult to replace.

I remember one day accompanying the executive on a round of supervision. When he got to the Supervisory Engineer's area, I noticed that several of the engineers were standing around a small radio, listening to a report on a football game. They didn't see us. When we left the area I asked my companion what his reaction had been.

THE ABSENT SUPERVISOR

"Darn it," he replied, "every time their boss is in his office these fellows manage to waste a little time here and there."

"Why is he in his office so much?" I asked.

"Oh, that's his concept of how to do his job. He claims he's got so much to do he can't get away from his office."

"Well, why don't you go in right now and ask him to see for himself what we've just happened on?"

"Oh, I can't do that. He'll get annoyed, tell me that his men get the work done all right, and assure me that he has to allow them their own way of doing things. If I press him too hard, he's liable to quit."

The Opposite Attitude

Paul Dubrow was Production Manager for a manufacturing company. He had four superintendents under him, each of whom controlled, on the average, seven foremen.

I went the rounds with Paul one day. While we were in a component-assembly department, Paul observed that two work areas were undermanned. Asking me to come with him, he turned right around and went to the office of the superintendent of that department.

THE DIRECT APPROACH

Paul told the superintendent what he'd discovered and asked him whether he'd known of the situation. The superintendent admitted ignorance, but said he'd investigate at once. Paul said he wanted an oral report from the superintendent within fifteen minutes, including an explanation of why there'd been an insufficient number of operators at the two tables, and what was being done to remedy the deficiency.

Meanwhile, Paul and I went on to another work area, for further in-depth supervision by him. When the fifteen minutes were up, Paul and

I were back in his office, and so was the superintendent, with a satisfactory report.

Lack of Control

Vince Lawton had the right idea about supervision. You'd always find him with his line subordinates, checking up on their progress and showing his sincere interest in them.

The only trouble was that Vince couldn't restrain himself. If he saw something he didn't like, he'd give vent to his displeasure and shout out what he wanted done immediately to rectify the situation. It didn't matter whether the culprit was alone or surrounded by others.

Vince's complaints weren't always justified, and many cases he thought emergencies were really not that urgent.

We finally straightened Vince out, especially after he lost a number of good men who couldn't and wouldn't take his unjustifiable method of criticizing and correcting them.

A Better Way

From the standpoint of tact and subtlety in followup, no one could beat Bruno Wilcox.

Bruno, too, was always engaged in the proper amount and kind of supervision. But Bruno was a very patient, calm and self-controlled man.

When conditions required him to make suggestions on the spot, for improvement, Bruno did so—privately and circumspectly.

But, aside from emergency situations, Bruno limited his supervisory remarks to words of encouragement and questions intended for finding out what was going on. Whenever possible, he refrained from commenting right then and there on any corrections or criticisms he wanted to make. He waited until shortly afterward, when he'd had time to think through more carefully what he wanted to say, and how he wanted to express it.

FOLLOWUP ACTION AWAY FROM SUPERVISED AREAS

In cases where it's feasible and desirable, here are some of the activities you can undertake *after* leaving the area where you've been visiting:

1. *Documentation:* First and foremost, *document* everything significant that you've observed or otherwise learned from your visit. There are some very definite ground rules for documenting effectively, including the following:

a. When in doubt about whether or not to record a particular item, document it. You never know when you may need to refer to it. Don't limit yourself to making note *only* of those things which you are *sure* you'll need again.

b. Avoid making notes for documentation purposes in the presence of subordinates. To do so is to cause them to worry unnecessarily. It's okay to make note of things you're willing to have the person read as you write them down, but don't use the *act* of documentation as an instrument for threatening or disciplining people. It doesn't pay off. Besides, there are more effective ways of applying warnings and discipline.

c. Just as soon as possible *after* you've left the area where you've been supervising, make notes—unobserved by others—of those facts or opinions you don't want to forget. You can transfer these notes later, in your office, to a more permanent record.

d. The first chance you get, in your office—when you're alone, record pertinent facts and opinions resulting from your supervision. Use a notebook—not looseleaf, in case you have to convince an arbitrator or judge in some future case that the notes were made at the time indicated—and keep that notebook *only* for such entries. Make all entries in chronological sequence, legibly (though in long hand). If you want to have a cross reference for any item, by person's name, you can set up a suitable system and note in it that you've written a particular thing about a specific person in your *documentation* book under a given date. If you want to have an active note referring to a Documentation-Book entry, you can put it in your tickler.

e. When you document, include not only *adverse* comments, but also *favorable* observations about the people supervised. Note the date, time and place of each comment. Include the names of people involved. And, as nearly as you remember them, state the facts and opinions you gleaned from your visits.

f. Keep on making pertinent entries in your Documentation Book, but don't show it to anyone unless it's *really* advisable to do so. You may want to establish the validity of an evaluation in your boss's mind by pointing to an entry in your Book. Or, as suggested above, you may have to prove a point in an arbitration or court case. But otherwise, that Book is between you and yourself, to help you form valid judgments and remember past situations having a bearing on the present.

2. *Decisions:* In cases where it's either unnecessary or inadvisable to reach conclusions or make decisions while among the people being supervised, meet this responsibility at the first possible moment when you're in your office. With your Documentation Book before you, you can think through what you observed and heard on your visit, weigh all the factors, and come to specific conclusions and/or decisions. Then make active note of any followup you deem advisable. *And,* round out your documentation with the conclusions or decisions you've arrived at.

3. *Steps involving commendation, reward or advancement:*
    a. Make, and document, your observations, conclusions and/or decisions about the people eligible for this kind of followup.
    b. Arrange to praise, commend, reward, recommend, promote or advance those deserving it.
    c. Arrange for further observation, communication or supervision in order to evaluate specific men as part of your overall program for knowing *who* qualifies for *what* benefit.
    d. Praise or commend those meriting it, make appropriate recommendations, and/or notify those involved of any promotion, advancement or reward which they've been granted.

4. *Steps involving improvement, correction, additional help, discipline, transfer or dismissal:*
    a. Come to pertinent conclusions and/or decisions about this kind of followup, and document them. Document, also, any followup action taken as a result of those conclusions or decisions.
    b. Apply any one or more of the following measures to those meriting them, making sure to do so privately:
      —Criticism.
      —Correction.
      —Suggestions or recommendations for improvement.
      —Guidance, help or advice.
      —A statement or re-statement of orders, instructions and/or standards to be met.
      —Training.
      —An explanation or re-explanation of facilities which are to be used properly.
      —Motivation.
    c. Issue pertinent warnings.
    d. For those meriting it, take proper steps to effect a change in duties, a transfer, discipline, and/or separation. Give appropriate notification to those involved.

FOLLOW UP IN DEPTH

You've already urged your subordinates to practice effective *supervision* in depth. Here's what you must do now:

- Emphasize the fact that all supervision must have effective followup.
- Describe the kind of followup you'd like to see, all the way down, through Front-Line Management.
- Impress on your immediate subordinates that they must see to it, through the proper channels, that all of *their* subordinate management men exercise proper followup on their own supervision.
- As you carry out your own supervision in depth, note any cases—on any level—where followup is not up to snuff. Point this out to those of your immediate subordinates who are involved, and check up later to see whether they've improved the situation to your satisfaction.

SUCCESS CAPSULE NUMBER SIXTEEN

In this *Success Factor* I took up the following points:

1. You must follow up on all supervision, and then check up again on whether your first followup actions were effective.
2. There are circumstances which make it advisable to take certain followup steps while physically present among the people being supervised.
3. In all other cases, it's wise to initiate the followup activities *away* from the people supervised, as soon as possible after leaving them.
4. One of the most important followup activities—to be carried out privately—is *documentation*. Document carefully and completely all matters to which you may wish or need to refer at some later time.
5. Make all necessary decisions growing out of your supervision, and carry them out as soon as practicable.
6. Take all appropriate steps for praising and/or rewarding those who merit it, or warning or disciplining those who warrant such treatment.
7. Right after supervision comes followup. Right after followup comes more supervision in order to check up on the followup. Then must come more followup. And so on, until the matter or situation in question is finally resolved satisfactorily.
8. Make sure that all of your subordinates engage in the proper kind of followup, all the way down the management line.